THEOLOGICAL INVESTIGATIONS

Volume XXII

THEOLOGICAL INVESTIGATIONS

VOLUME XXII
HUMANE SOCIETY AND
THE CHURCH OF TOMORROW

by

KARL RAHNER

Translated by

JOSEPH DONCEEL, S.J.

CROSSROAD • NEW YORK

1991

The Crossroad Publishing Company
370 Lexington Avenue, New York, NY 10017

A translation of the first three sections of *Schriften zur Theologie, XVI*
Copyright © 1984 by Benziger Verlag
Zürich, Einsiedeln, Köln

Printed in the United States of America
Typesetting output: TEXSource, Houston

Library of Congress Catalog Card Number: 61-8189
ISBN 0-8245-0924-2

CONTENTS

PART ONE *Humane Society*

PART TWO *Ecumenism*

PART THREE *The Future of the Church*

PART ONE

Humane Society

1

CONSCIENCE

FREEDOM AND THE DIGNITY OF HUMAN DECISION

Despite many necessary reservations theology is convinced that it has said the ultimately decisive thing about conscience. In doing so theology is aware that theological statements as such tend to introduce conscience into the mystery that we call God. And thus theological statements unavoidably take on some of the vagueness and obscurity that belong to religious language.

THE MANY QUESTIONS
THAT MAY AND SHOULD BE ASKED

There are many aspects of the problem which I do not intend to discuss. Here are a few of them: What the Old Testament has to say about conscience, which it called the "heart"; how conscience refers to God, as mentioned already in the Old Testament; what Jesus taught about conscience, which he too called the heart; how the technical term for "conscience" (*syneidesis*), deriving from popular Stoic philosophy and already adopted in everyday language during the first century, entered Christian literature in Paul's letters; how this notion was transformed by early Christianity; what the Fathers of the Church (e.g., Tertullian, Origen, Chrysostom, and especially Augustine) taught about conscience; what medieval theology said about it, especially as, starting in the twelfth century, it commented on a text of Jerome about *synteresis* and *conscientia*;

3

how medieval theology understood with Thomas that an invincibly erroneous conscience remains validly normative;[1] against a secularized conception of conscience that tends to emphasize moral autonomy as opposed to the theonomy of conscience, to uphold the conviction that conscience refers to God; how the idea of conscience continued to develop in Christian theology through new insights coming from modern psychology and depth psychology, sociology and ethnology, leading to the admission of freedom of conscience and religion, as happened for the Catholic Church in the Second Vatican Council. Such are the topics that I cannot discuss here, without implying that they are not important for the theology of conscience.

Likewise many points cannot be brought up which the theologian should say about non-theological theories of conscience. Thus we cannot speak of the fact that conscience cannot be explained by admitting the existence of inborn moral ideas. There will be no explicit confrontation with Kant's description of conscience as a transcendental power. We cannot explicitly speak of the origin of the superego according to the psychology of Freud. No explicit evaluation need be expected of the findings of modern existential philosophy, of ethology, of ethnology, of biological evolutionism, and so on. It stands to reason that theology does not ignore all the contributions of the modern anthropological sciences that are important for a full understanding of what is meant by conscience. Of course, there is a development of conscience; of course, it is in part conditioned by biological ways of behaving, for which ethologists discover analogies among animals. Of course, early childhood shows a development of conscience, with all the antecedents and factors of such development. Of course, the concrete formation of conscience is conditioned biologically, sociologically, and culturally by the orders and prohibitions which that formation itself imposes. Of course, we do not clearly discover in the history of prehistoric humanity, cultures, and civilizations any clear and verbalized knowledge of the theonomous nature of conscience. Nor is it possible, even today, to explain it quickly to everybody. But, as we said, we cannot discuss all of this here, because if we did

---

[1]S. Th., 1, 2, q. 19a. 5; *De ver.*, q. 17a. 4 ad 2. Cf. Rudolf Hofmann, "Die Gewissenslehre des Walter von Brügge O.F.M. und die Entwicklung der Gewissenslehre in der Hochscholastik,"*Beiträge zur Geschichte der Philosophie und Theologie des Mittelalters* XXXVI/5–6 (Münster 1941), esp. 145–204.

we would be unable to explain thoroughly and clearly enough that which interests the theologian about this topic. I mean the relation that exists between conscience and God.

STARTING FROM THE ERRONEOUS CONSCIENCE

I do not intend to use here the method of a transcendental reflection on the nature of conscience as the unconditional way in which the spirit accepts its freedom. Let me start rather from a quite different consideration, even if at first it seems to be secondary. I will try to reflect on the absolutely binding character of what is called an erroneous conscience.

The Absolutely Binding Character of the Dictates of Conscience

It will soon be evident that, terminologically, it is a mistake to speak of an erroneous conscience. But for the time being this hardly matters.

No ethics, regardless of how radically "objective" it may be, can ever forego subjective human consciousness, because objective moral norms and the objective relationship that exists between freedom and God, which renders the individual norms absolute, become present only through the intermediary of a personal decision of conscience. In other words, even the norms of morality that are considered most objective must appeal to human freedom in order to become real and effective for freedom. Moral norms and commands can become effective only when they are known and understood. Therefore a subjective judgment is a last court of appeal beyond which there can be no other. Objective norms have to be grasped as absolutely binding. That is why a dictate of conscience is absolutely binding for a decision of human freedom.

This is not an endorsement of arbitrary subjectivism. Human beings are obliged to harmonize their knowledge with objective reality, as presented to them, and to accept it as a norm. Theoretically, all those who have the use of their intelligence admit this obligation, since they cannot avoid conforming their knowledge to the reality that forces itself upon them. And so all persons know at least implicitly, but really, that before they make a decision they must look for information and be guided by the reality of objective morality. They know that they cannot act as they please nor make up the laws of their conduct; they know that they must, to the best of their ability and knowledge, submit wholeheartedly to the rules of objective morality. This shows that not every opinion, every preference, every arbitrary prejudice can claim to be a real dictate of conscience. Yet it is true that in situations where people must make decisions and act within the framework of their possibilities, after having given the alternatives sufficient thought, if they reach the conclusion that one of the alternatives is the right one, then their decision is absolutely binding on them. It is a dictate of conscience that obliges them absolutely.

We do not treat explicitly the problem of what people should consider their duty when, in a doubtful case, they feel unable to conclude clearly which of two possible answers is the right one. In such a perplexing case, when there is a lack of conclusive grounds for deciding, and a decision has to be taken, and no greater practical clarity can be reached, we say then that either of the two possibilities is morally acceptable.

So henceforth we will take it for granted that, where a choice has to be made, our decision is a dictate of conscience, if it looks absolutely binding to the subject.

Erroneous Conscience

Before we inquire further what is implied in such a decision, which imposes upon subjects and their freedom an absolute responsibility that cannot be transferred to anybody or anything else, we must keep in mind that even such a decision of conscience can, in a sense that has to be further explained, be an erroneous one. The possibility of an erroneous yet binding dictate of conscience is admitted by Christian moral theology, at least by Thomas Aquinas, and it has revealed its radical consequences in the texts of Vatican II on freedom of conscience and of religion. It has taken the Church a long time to reach this insight, because the doctrine of the possibility of an erroneous decision of conscience is not as obvious as we may think. And also because nowadays almost everyone is inclined to present even pet opinions, which one is unwilling to defend too strenuously, as dictates of conscience. But Christian moral theology does admit that people's opinions about their concrete moral conduct may be erroneous and, at the same time, real dictates of conscience that oblige them absolutely and render them personally responsible. This case is far from obvious. A person's moral judgment may be erroneous, may truly contradict the objective order of values, and yet also be a real self-understanding of the subject. That is evident. It happens everyday; everyone has encountered such cases. We are often mistaken, even in the field of moral values. But that such an erroneous judgment may nevertheless — not always, but often — be a genuine dictate of conscience; that it obliges the erring person absolutely; that, speaking as Christians, it is here and now for that person a command of God; that disobeying it would make the person be rejected by God; that a judgment whose content is morally false may nonetheless constitute a categorical imperative whose transgression would render the person evil — all of this is not obvious.

There are several ways of showing why it is not obvious. One might point out that the moral non-values to which this judgment refers cannot constitute a positive moral injunction for the subject, so that a real dictate of conscience would be excluded. One might say that a dictate of conscience concerning a obligation sent from God cannot oblige one to something that God positively rejects and orders us to avoid. One might say that a moral non-value, unlike a moral value in its absolute sovereignty, cannot give rise to the unconditional decisiveness that belongs to the nature of a dictate of conscience. Yet Christian moral theology as well as human and Christian opinion hold that there are such dictates of conscience, although error and absolute obligation seem to be totally contradictory concepts that cannot coexist in the same reality. Yet according to Vatican II, "conscience frequently errs from invincible ignorance without losing its dignity" (*Gaudium et Spes*, 16). How does it not lose its dignity when it errs?

The Dignity of a Dictate of Conscience

This question can be answered only when one sees that, even in the event of an erroneous decision of conscience, a person performs an act that is founded in the positive dignity and binding character of a dictate of conscience. This dignity and binding character cannot be situated in the categorical object (some moral value or non-value), but must derive from elsewhere, if we are to explain the binding character of even an erroneous dictate of conscience. How is this possible? We can answer this question only by examining the nature and structure of a decision of conscience.

The absolute dignity and obligation of a dictate of conscience does not come properly and solely from the single categorical concrete value with which it is concerned. Why would a single human life, which is perishable after all, be able to demand for itself the absolute right to be respected? How can individuals demand, on the basis of their insignificant reality, that their person be respected in absolute fidelity and love? Where can two persons by themselves alone find a basis for a demand of absolute honesty and integrity in their dealings with each other?

If one wishes to achieve a goal, one must use the necessary means to reach it. If a number of people wish to live peacefully together, some rules will have to be observed. But all these considerations remain hypothetical. They always assume the following form: *If* you do not want to harm your liver, use alcohol with moderation. But do I personally have to want my liver to stay healthy? Are health, peace, and some kind of happiness values that must be *unconditionally* achieved? Once more: The world of concrete realities and values, to which binding decisions of conscience refer, cannot by itself alone justify such an absolute claim. So, if such claims exist, their absolute and obligatory character must come from elsewhere.

If there exists a more basic and general source of obligation, prior to all individual values, we see right away that this source of absolute moral claims can be effective also in an erroneous conscience, one that errs about individual concrete realities, without erring about the foundation of their absolute claim. In other words: In both the right *and* the erroneous decision of conscience, despite their disagreement about the concrete moral value, one and the same basic moral reality is at work. The error refers only to the concrete data, not to what bestows upon them their absolute obligation. That is why the concept "erroneous conscience" is a misnomer. There are no truly erroneous dictates of conscience. If there were, they would not be dictates of conscience because they would not claim an absolute obligation.

The Transcendental Ground of the Absolute Claim

What is the foundation of the absolute character of morality prior to the actual appeal of particular values? This has not yet been made clear by the preceding discussion. In order to answer that question we must go back to what was hinted at above, before we considered the problem of erroneous conscience.

In every dictate of conscience, including the so-called erroneous one, we affirm and accept as unconditionally evident that fundamental and permanent distinction between good and evil, between what ought and what ought not to be, whether or not this distinction is also affirmed for the immediate object of our activity. Every dictate of conscience affirms this basic distinction as permanent. Just as every judgment affirms the principle of contradiction as universally valid and ineradicable, so that even its very denial reaffirms it, thus acknowledging its transcendental necessity, so a dictate of conscience that refers to a free action asserts the transcendental necessity of the distinction between good and evil. Even those who say explicitly that in dictates of conscience this basic distinction is relative and can be denied and ignored would, in their denial, implicitly maintain that their own judgment is valid and the only absolutely correct norm for their freedom. In other words, a transcendental experience of freedom and responsibility does exist, and it cannot be one datum among others within our consciousness. Empirical psychological reflection may, absolutely speaking, reduce every single datum to another one, so that it is unable to discover freedom and responsibility. But still there exists a transcendental experience of our being free and responsible subjects. It is still there when one calls it in doubt, when one is unable to discover it as one datum among others in spatio-temporal experience. One may try to run away from one's freedom and responsibility and interpret oneself as a product of others, of non-I's. But even this self-interpretation is the action of the subject as such. It is an action by which the subject denies itself or interprets its freedom as an enslavement to the arbitrary whim of something alien. It is a self-interpretation that misses its self. Yet in this very action one acts as a free subject and reveals oneself as such in the very misinterpretation. It is a mistake to confuse that which one affirms in this interpretation (the absence of freedom) with the fact of affirming it, the affirmed with the affirming. Of course, the undeniable fact that we are responsible for ourselves is always mediated by some concrete object. But with this mediation, which is not identical with our transcendental self-responsibility, we experience our freedom and genuine responsibility, that is, our conscience. It is an unconditional appeal addressed to me, as a responsible subject; the response to the appeal is up to my freedom, not to my whim. For even if the subject in freedom refuses to heed it, the appeal continues to live in the refusal. All this occurs whenever a person errs about concrete data. That is why every real decision of conscience is to be accepted as an absolute summons to freedom and responsibility, even when it is "erroneous."

Conscience As God's Voice

What are the further implications of this unavoidable transcendental self-givenness of the subject to itself in freedom and responsibility? One becomes a subject only on account of the transcendentality of the spirit and of freedom, both of them unlimited, because of the subject's openness for being as such and in its totality. Without such unlimited transcendentality the subject cannot be really self-possessed and free. Such an unlimited transcendentality implies what we may call the person's dynamic reaching to the infinite and unfathomable Mystery, to God, who is anonymously affirmed whenever unlimited transcendentality with it ensuing freedom and responsibility is accepted. Thus, it is possible to explain the theonomous nature of conscience.

When one interprets conscience as the voice of God, one is basically right. For this does not mean that God intrudes miraculously into our consciousness as a concrete datum. Nor does it mean that the judgment needed in a decision of conscience is always and necessarily right about the concrete reality to which it refers. It means that in every decision of conscience, even in an erroneous one, there arise an absolute obligation and the responsibility of freedom that subjects can reject only by destroying themselves. Such a decision always and necessarily implies an affirmation of God.

The Freedom of Conscience

By interpreting conscience as a reference to God we understand the principal text of Vatican II about conscience, although that text is formulated in religious language. It reads:

> In the depths of his conscience, man detects a law which he does not impose upon himself, but which holds him to obedience. Always summoning him to love good and avoid evil, the voice of conscience can when necessary speak to his heart more specifically: do this, shun that. For man has in his heart a law written by God. To obey it is the very dignity of man; according to it he will be judged.
>
> Conscience is the most secret core and sanctuary of a man. There he is alone with God, whose voice echoes in his depths. In a wonderful manner conscience reveals that law which is fulfilled by love of God and neighbor. In fidelity to conscience, Christians are joined with the rest of men in the search for truth, and for the genuine solution to the numerous problems which arise in the life of individuals and from social relationships. Hence the more that a correct conscience holds sway, the more persons and groups turn aside from blind choice and strive to be guided by objective norms of morality.
>
> Conscience frequently errs from invincible ignorance without losing its dignity. The same cannot be said of a man who cares but little for truth and goodness, or of a conscience which by degrees grows practically sightless as a result of habitual sin. (*Gaudium et Spes*, 16 in *The Documents of Vatican II*, edited by Walter Abbott)

There is no need to interpret this text of the Council in more detail. Attention should be drawn, however, to a few points that follow from this understanding of the nature of conscience, especially to what today is called freedom of conscience and of religion. Through their conscience human beings are real subjects; they may not be treated like objects. Conscience must be respected by all social and ecclesiastical authorities, since their immediate function concerns the objective structures of reality. One's freedom of conscience and of religion should not infringe upon that of others because this would constitute what is usually called a violation of the common good. This brings up further questions about conflicts between freedom of conscience and the common good, that is, the freedom of others. We cannot discuss these questions here.

No wonder that, in this respect, the Church's doctrine and practice have undergone developments and changes.

Both society and the Church have the right and the duty to teach people about objective norms of morality and to exhort them to observe these norms. In other words: They teach the right way of applying conscience to concrete realities. This does not infringe upon freedom of conscience. The increasing complexity of the human situation and people's activities, both individually and collectively, renders it quite difficult to decide exactly for any concrete case what is objectively true or false. In defending human rights, neither the Church nor society can give up its right to present and defend norms of objective morality. But the Church at least would be well advised if she concentrated her efforts in another direction: namely, to point out more clearly that humanity strives irresistibly for God and that, in this striving, human morality becomes theonomous and, as a result, really autonomous.

It is good and practically indispensable to hold as morally binding and to obey the concrete everyday obligations that make life in society tolerable. But if people are not aware of the exalted dignity of conscience, of the individual's ultimate responsibility before God, or one's irresistible yearning for God, all objective morality and every instance of living up to it would, in the final analysis, be nothing but a higher kind of dog training that is unworthy of human dignity and unworthy of God. To put it a bit too strongly, but in fact correctly, one might say: A dictate of conscience that errs about concrete morality is more important and wonderful than an objectively correct "dictate of conscience" (not really one at all) that would neither explicitly nor implicitly affirm in freedom the transcendental dimension that refers to God.

In instances where one party must presume the presence of a real decision of conscience in another party, they have something in common before God, although there may exist a contradiction in the material content of their decisions, with the result that either one (or often perhaps both) could be false. Should both sides really understand this, should they be aware that before God and in God's grace they share a bond that is more important than bitter discord about the material content of their conscientious decisions, they might develop a genuine tolerance that surpasses by far what is meant by tolerance in the social and political arena. Bitter quarrels about lofty human values and goods may not be considered innocuous; they should not lead to cheap compromises. Rather they are founded in the luminous peace for which every genuine decision of conscience strives, however bitter may be the feud that in such cases we have to endure for the sake of conscience.

2

DIALOGUE AND TOLERANCE
AS THE FOUNDATION OF
A HUMANE SOCIETY

Dialogue and tolerance as the foundation of a humane society sounds at first rather problematic. When one declares that one reality is the foundation of another, one generally presupposes two things: that one has a clear and distinct idea of the second reality, which needs a foundation; and that the first reality, which is clearly distinct from the second, is absolutely presupposed by the latter. But if one understands the title of this article, the first presupposition becomes very doubtful. When is a society "humane"?

At the time of the Reformation a ruler who expelled subjects unwilling to share his religion, and who refused dialogue and rejected religious tolerance, might have said that this was the only way to establish and protect a humane society in his country, because only a society that belonged to his denomination, which he considered the true one, could be really humane in all respects. For such a ruler the refusal of open dialogue and the practice of intolerance would have been the unconditional presupposition of a humane society. On closer inspection one would have to say that all fascist and radically socialist regimes share this opinion, because they are convinced that, in the final analysis, philosophical intolerance makes for the actual happiness of the greatest number in a society, and thus for real humanism. That is why they defend their political and social ideology not only with logical arguments but also with intolerance and compulsion, through censorship, removal from office, and so on.

So when we say that dialogue and tolerance are the foundation of a humane society, we presuppose, contrary to the opinion or conviction of others around us, a society whose essential features include dialogue and tolerance. That is why we readily grant that the title of this article contains a tautology. A society is humane only if it allows the widest possible tolerance in social dialogue. And the other way around: Dialogue and tolerance characterize a humane society; it cannot exist without them.

At this point even those who, without hesitation, define a humane society as one characterized by dialogue and tolerance should be cautious. The history of human societies shows clearly that what people mean by dialogue and tolerance has not always been exactly the same. A Greek *polis* considered itself a seat of freedom and dialogue, although it held as obvious that an economy without slaves was impossible and that it had the right to condemn a Socrates to death, on account of ungodliness. Throughout the centuries the freedom of the Christian has been extolled. Yet, when we measure it with our standards, the history of Christianity has been, to a dreadful extent, a history of intolerance, of persecution of heretics, of wars of religion, and of coercion of conscience by leaders of Church and State.

LIMITS OF DIALOGUE AND TOLERANCE — THE COMMON GOOD

It is precisely this history that saddens the Christian and the humanist, that warns us to be prudent and moderate. Today can we always welcome dialogue? Are we supposed never to terminate or to interrupt it except when the parties have reached an agreement? Is it possible in public life to forego every decision that does not translate a general consensus reached through dialogue? Who has the last word and declares that everything has been sufficiently "thrashed out"? Can a dialogue ever reach an end by itself alone? And again, is it possible in every instance to be tolerant in one's dealings with others?

It is often said (also in modern church declarations as in those of Vatican II) that the tolerance one should harbor for the freedom of others has its limits in the common good, which may not be harmed. Nowadays efforts are being made to eliminate from the idea of the common good certain elements that derive from religious beliefs and, from the start, to use this secularized idea of the common good to do away with whatever may lead to religious discord. Are these efforts successful? Is it, for instance, a blatant case of intolerance when some state legislatures in the United States forbid the teaching of evolution in the public schools? Is it a violation of tolerance and the equal rights of an atheistic philosophy when in West Germany the state universities have theological faculties but no faculty whose task it would be to develop a radically atheistic critique of religion?

But even if one was to admit that in our modern progressive society there are still remnants of intolerance to be eliminated, the question would remain what exactly is meant by the common good and who is to decide on its meaning. For even in the most progressive and tolerant society, the common good continues to have the right and the duty to defend itself against encroachments by individuals, without the consent of these individuals. It has the right to be intolerant, if one wishes to define intolerance as treating the freedom of others in a way that they do not approve. So if, on account of the common good, such restriction of freedom is simply unavoidable, and if in this sense intolerance cannot be completely avoided and is in fact not being avoided in any society whatsoever, who determines the common good that legitimates such intolerance?

In a society where (except for a few offenders) there exists no real difference of opinion about the common good, the above question does not arise. If, on the other hand, there exist serious differences of opinion even about the fundamental questions of the common good, how does one then determine the range of dialogue and tolerance as well as its unavoidable limits? True, the genuine conception of the common good is itself one that changes in the course of history; society must continually revise it. But this constant revision burdens the individual human mind and especially the moral conscience with the burning question of what standards to use and what direction to follow in order to live up to its responsibility. At the same time, the idea of the common good, the idea of possible dialogue and of tolerance, are in a process of continual revision.

What degree of tolerance in open dialogue should one favor, if one cannot simply admit that there should be no limits to one's readiness for dialogue and tolerance? One may, for instance, be morally opposed to abortion, while admitting in a discussion that such an action should not fall under the penal law. A dialogue may present the opportunity to discuss the question of whether the abettors of a voluntary suicide should be prosecuted. However, the Nazi regime, for instance, did things and imposed burdens that are to be rejected out of hand, that are no fitting topic for tolerant dialogue among people who consider each other equally intelligent and humane, even though they disagree about practical matters.

If therefore it is not so easy to explain exactly what is meant by the willingness to welcome dialogue and tolerance, and to explain what it does not include, it is not so simple to divide people into those who are for and those who are against dialogue and tolerance. A sober appraisal of human reality and history will have to grant that there will always be disagreement about the nature of real humanism, hence also about the correct idea of tolerance and willingness to dialogue.

At this rather dim point of our reflections one might wonder whether the point on which all people might agree would not be that they should acknowledge this situation and welcome the greatest possible tolerance and openness to dialogue. But there will be no unanimity about this conclusion either. There will always be those who claim that at times one must force others to reach happiness. This idea of a legitimate intolerance undoubtedly prevails in modern Muslim nations and socialist countries. In both of them an official ideology is imposed on all, and efforts are made to carry it out even if individuals do not agree.

The proponents of such official ideologies might of course reply to us "Westerners," that we too would restrict our tolerance by appealing to an indefinable common good. We would differ from intolerant official ideologies only in our different conceptions of the common good. We of the tolerant West would answer that our idea of the common good is wider, more tolerant, and, therefore, more correct than that of these State ideologies, because freedom, hence also tolerance, is preferable to a common good and a general happiness imposed by force from above. To us in the West that view seems quite obvious, since we cannot conceive of a genuine common good without the greatest possible amount of freedom for the individual, a freedom which is itself an essential element of human well being.

But the other side might inquire whether the amount of tolerance favored by us does not seriously threaten the common good that all have to strive for, so that this threat to the common good would amount to a serious threat to freedom. We might be asked by the other side whether the common good, as we understand it, is not reduced by an exaggerated tolerance to the function of a mere economy of consumption, an inhuman economy headed for absurdity.

These considerations show how problematic are the idea and the ideal of tolerance. It is impossible to conceive of tolerance as wholly independent of the common good. The latter brings up the metaphysical question of the exact nature of the common good. It brings up a social and political problem: How does a given society at a given time envision the longed for reconciliation between the freedom of individuals and groups, on the one hand, and the limits which the structure of society necessarily imposes on that freedom, on the other? This reconciliation cannot be reached once and for all but is a part of ongoing history. So the question which interests both individuals and groups is how real reconciliation in a given society, situation, and period of history will be reached, and whether this society is really determined to stand by it in the future. We in the West will, I hope, resolutely cling to what we call our "free self-government," although we must keep in mind that this free self-government with its concrete tolerance needs to be further developed and that tolerance is not the only and absolute standard of our existence.

TOLERANCE AS REQUIRED BY CHRISTIANITY

We must now consider the nature of tolerance from another point of view, which will better show how thoroughly Christian and how radical the demand for tolerance is. Let us start by insisting once more that, as we show how Christian the radical demand for tolerance is, we do not at all imply that Christianity and the Church have, during the two thousand years of their history, always practiced the tolerance that is demanded by the Christian conception of humanity. To a frightful extent the opposite has very often been the case. We must not forget that a reality in history discovers and realizes itself very slowly. There is always some contradiction between what it is and what it ought to be. But our task here is neither to attack nor to defend the churches' record in the matter of tolerance.

We are speaking rather of the tolerance that should exist, that is demanded by a basic understanding of human freedom, such as it exists in Christians and is available to all. In a short article we cannot, of course, develop a metaphysical and Christian anthropology. Hence we start from an idea that belongs, or should belong, to every kind of humanism. In a lengthy process of spiritual growth Christianity and the churches have painfully discovered that tolerance is part of the Christian message. We mean the idea that even the invincibly erroneous conscience constitutes an unconditional moral demand, to which persons owe unconditional obedience before themselves and before God, and with which nobody has a right to interfere. Hence there arises a demand for tolerance that stands far above all utilitarian considerations about peace or peaceful coexistence in a society of various individuals and opinions.

THE ERRONEOUS CONSCIENCE

We start from the idea that even an invincibly erroneous conscience constitutes an unconditional moral duty, to which persons owe, before themselves and before God, an unconditional obedience. We are not inquiring here how the absolute dictate of conscience should be interpreted metaphysically and theologically. Neither are we inquiring how an unconditional moral obligation should be interpreted or even whether or not it should be interpreted. We are not asking whether or not one should stop at a categorical imperative as an ultimate datum of human existence and freedom, or whether one explains this obligation through a previous knowledge about God and God's will, or whether it is precisely from the unconditionality of moral duty that we begin to understand what is meant by God. As a Christian theologian I am allowed to presuppose that the unconditionality of a moral duty has something to do with the one we call God, without having to try to clarify the connection. In any case, we take for granted that there exist absolute obligations in human existence, which cannot be reduced to psychological, utilitarian, or sociological factors.

Granting therefore that the dictate of conscience possesses this ultimate unconditionality even when it is objectively erroneous, we must first make it clear that not every opinion, every preference, every arbitrary prejudice that people hold and about which they are at least implicitly aware that they are unjustified in holding, can claim to be a dictate of conscience, especially since such opinions are not held with the full commitment of one's existence.

Yet the following statement is still true. When in a given situation persons have to act, and when, to the extent of their possibilities, they reach a decision which they consider true and morally right, and preferable to another available one, this judgment is binding for them; it is a dictate of conscience that is absolutely obliging.

But everyday experience shows that according to objective norms such a judgment may in fact be erroneous. Yet a judgment that is factually erroneous can be a real dictate of conscience that is absolutely binding on a person. This doctrine of the possibility of an erroneous yet absolutely binding dictate of conscience has — albeit only slowly and with all the implied consequences — been generally admitted in Christian moral theology at least since Thomas Aquinas and has, in a slow learning process of the Church, led to radical consequences for freedom of conscience and of religion, as was evidenced in Vatican II.

It is not as obvious as we tend to feel today that it is possible for a decision to come from one's inner existence and to constitute an absolutely binding decision of conscience, even though that decision is wrong. Today people are too prone to present as a decision of conscience their favorite opinions that they are unwilling to justify in a radical way. But current Christian moral theology admits such a possibility, and this with respect to *all* possible objects of such a decision of conscience. This means (once more): One's judgment concerning one's concrete moral attitude and decision may be wrong and still be a real, radical decision of conscience that obliges one absolutely in an inescapable responsibility, in which the innermost nature of a radically free decision is realized.

This is not an obvious platitude. Everyday life and our individual experience show that we are often wrong, even in the domain of moral values. What is not obvious is that such a judgment can nevertheless be a genuine dictate of conscience with its absolute obligation, so that ignoring it makes one guilty in God's eyes and renders one evil. Yet Christian moral theology as well as human and Christian life-experience insist on the fact that such erroneous, yet absolutely obliging, dictates of conscience may occur in a person's concrete situation, although error and absolute obligation seem to be utterly contradictory notions. "Conscience frequently errs from invincible ignorance without losing its dignity," says the Second Vatican Council (*Gaudium et Spes*, 16).

We will have to forego a more detailed explanation of why and how such a decision imposes an absolute obligation, in spite of the error about its immediate object. We can only say that a definite moral decision, in which persons realize their definitive desire of the absolute good and their definitive stance as free subjects, can occur, even through the intermediary of the categorical object of such a decision, which objectively and in itself is not legitimate.

ACKNOWLEDGING THE DIGNITY OF FREEDOM

What is important for our topic is this: What we usually call tolerance is not only a maxim for peaceful coexistence, in which people with different opinions and goals get along without harming each other physically. It is rather the respect we pay to the freedom of other persons as they make their decisions of conscience. These decisions are absolutely binding on them, even when we believe, rightly perhaps, that they are wrong. Because a decision of conscience is absolutely binding, even when in fact it is wrong, it represents an absolute (we do not say infinite) value that must be respected by the person who has made the decision.

During the Council many who opposed the Council's teaching on freedom of religion declared that error has no rights. The defenders of freedom of religion were right when they answered: Error in itself has no rights, but erring people do. For such a factually wrong dictate of conscience still stands for the dignity of conscience, the dignity of freedom, the dignity of each individual's personal responsibility, which one can neither shake off nor transfer to another, the dignity that everybody must respect. That is why tolerance is not merely a rule in a game played by realistic and intelligent people who want to get along with one another. It is an acknowledgment of the absolute dignity of the freedom and the personality of human beings. That dignity is still present in erroneous decisions of conscience. It would be rejected and denied if it were given up in behalf of the merely factual correctness of some piece of knowledge. It is precisely because a dictate of conscience may not simply be confused with a shallow opinion and yet may coexist with error that it took Christianity centuries of reflection before it was able to draw the ultimate consequences from the lofty dignity of even an erroneous conscience. It took Christianity a long time to discover that tolerance has something to do with the innermost nature of the human person as a free subject, that tolerance must be practiced even where it is not foisted on one by the physical power of one's opponents, even where nobody can prevent one from being intolerant. Intolerance cannot be practiced even when we are absolutely convinced that we are speaking for the truth and for the greater good of our opponents, because intolerance would eliminate or unduly restrict the freedom of others, without which they cannot be what they want to be or ought to be, namely, free persons, whose reality, as far as possible, is of their own making. Understood in this way tolerance derives from the human self-understanding that belongs both to Western humanism and to genuine Christianity. It is a tolerance that we would wish to be part of the self-understanding of all human beings.

TOLERANCE AND INTOLERANCE

But here the real problem of tolerance begins. Let us remember what was said in the first part of our reflections where tolerance was presented as a good that, although legitimate and desirable, is nevertheless limited by the common good of others. The common good does not allow everything to be tolerated in everybody. Tolerance has its limits, in view of the doctrine that in the common good the right of one person is restricted by the equal rights of others. In the second part of our considerations tolerance was seen as acknowledgment that there are possibilities of freedom which free subjects, on account of their dignity, require to be themselves and that a person's possibilities are not limited by others' possibilities of freedom, but are without limits.

Such tolerance necessarily engenders conflict because it postulates possibilities of freedom for one person that are, or may already be, preempted by another person. For these possibilities of different subjects are not separate, they overlap. And we cannot expect the common possibilities of freedom to be divided peacefully and naturally among free subjects in such a way that there is no conflict, that no one person claims more possibilities than another. The freedom supposed by tolerance, as mentioned in the second part of our reflections, is loaded with conflicts. The common good, the freedom of others, imposes limits on our freedom, which our freedom would not impose on itself if left alone.

The tolerance that lets itself be restricted by the common good is intolerant of the tolerance which free subjects demand spontaneously as their unrestricted right. Although we readily grant that free subjects spontaneously impose some essential norms on themselves, that they do not aim simply at unrestricted subjectivity, at the same time they will often be inclined to do things that they will find impossible to carry out because of the simple reality of the intolerance of others, which, prior to any ill will, imposes limits on the possibilities of others. Reality is not such that everything will always be harmonized.

These propositions have been put quite abstractly, so that the inexorable difficulty meant here may not be too quickly and too cheaply talked away. In their private and public lives people must often be intolerant toward one another, in order to show their tolerance by securing and protecting the possibilities of freedom of others. This bitter necessity is one of the factors of human existence, although it is frequently overlooked. Some people seem to bring off the trick of making everyone feel free without impairing the freedom of anyone else.

This unavoidable difficulty, that there can be no tolerance without some intolerance, that there really exists an intolerance that is a condition of generous tolerance, has another unpalatable aspect: There is no clear and handy criterion that would allow us to determine the exact dosage of tolerance and intolerance, of tolerance for one party and intolerance for the other, and the other way around. Who would be able to set up such a criterion? Is not the whole of human history with its unceasing conflicts between freedom and coercion, with its ceaseless efforts to combine the greatest possible freedom with the least possible coercion, not an ever new proof that there does not exist any handy criterion that will solve all conflicts?

True, from the second part of our remarks one may certainly deduce the maxim that there should be as much freedom and room for freedom as possible and as few instances of restricting and intolerant coercion as possible. But what is the meaning of "as much as possible" and "as few as possible," since freedom ought to exist and since coercion, which contradicts freedom, has to exist as well in order for there to be freedom? There is no such criterion. Should it exist, history would stop and vanish. Neither socialism, which openly wants to restrict everyone's possibilities of freedom and reconcile them in the name of the common good, nor an absolute liberalism, which would give total freedom to all parties, can serve as such a criterion. We cannot escape history, in which the concrete coexistence of freedom and necessity must always be determined ever anew and always in a different way. However, even if this situation cannot be changed, one thing is possible and, as shown above, is in agreement with human and Christian principles. It is also for us a duty for the future.

PRE-EMINENCE OF FREEDOM

The presumption favors freedom. There can exist unavoidable necessities, coercions, and restrictions of freedom. But in the final analysis they have to justify themselves before the bench of freedom, and not the other way around. People may be firmly of this mind. Whether they really are, or only expect others to be, while they themselves betray this maxim in their own attitudes and actions, can quite simply be found out from their answer to the following question: Are you really willing to grant freedom to the other person, insofar as it can be done without harming others, even when you hold a different opinion and have the power to prevent others from doing what they want? Are you willing and patient enough, as far as possible, to find out and to try to feel what others (or another group) want to be and how they want to understand themselves?

The sincere answer to this question with a genuine yes might show whether such tolerance and readiness for dialogue are at hand. But since this question too includes the condition "as far as possible," the sincerity of the answer is ultimately hidden in the solitude of the individual conscience that can be judged only by

God, although the effort must be made, in dialogue, to find out whether the answer was really honest. This allows the theologian to say that all persons will one day be judged before God about this point: whether they have really granted to their neighbor, individually and collectively, the freedom that is their inalienable and most personal right, whether they have in that sense been tolerant and willing to dialogue.

3

UTOPIA AND REALITY: THE SHAPE OF CHRISTIAN EXISTENCE CAUGHT BETWEEN THE IDEAL AND THE REAL

The combination of the words "utopia" and "reality" points to a basic dualism in human existence. Biologically humans have a lower and an upper, an inner and an outer, component. Their personal reality proceeds from a present that is the product of a past and moves toward a still to be realized future. By experiencing the given realities they discover the basic norms of their activity, by which they measure the positive or negative value of their reality. They speak of an earth and look forward to a heaven. They would like to be sober realists as well as persons who strive creatively for higher goals. Whether happy or unhappy, they measure their reality by standards that are distinct from it. Fortune and misfortune, success and failure, life and death, truth and error, and thousands of like dualisms show that they do not live in complete identity with themselves, that from countless points of view they exist as a unity that remains a diversity. No wonder then that the two words "utopia" and "reality" are juxtaposed and experienced in both their distinction and their mutual relationship.

THE DUALISM OF UTOPIA AND REALITY

But what is utopia? What do we mean by it? What is reality? Which one is meant here? And what have all these ideas and questions to do with the way Christians shape their life and their world? The words "ideal" and "reality" in the subtitle of this article should, for clarity's sake, be understood in the same sense as utopia and reality. What we are doing is to inquire about the Christian way of shaping life and the world, insofar as this shaping is caught between utopia and reality.

What do we mean here by utopia? This word, coined by St. Thomas More, should not be taken as referring to everything that has not yet been realized, and for which we keep striving, although reaching it is arduous, uncertain, and even unlikely. We beg to be allowed to understand utopia here as those goals and tasks that persons not only *can* but *ought* to strive for. As task and duty they stand unrealized before us, they seem to demand too much of us, they look as though they will never be realized.

Humanity seems to be burdened with countless such utopias. We want biological and social security, and we feel threatened and uncertain in our biological and economic existence. We want to *know*, that is, to get a *well-organized* picture of reality in our minds, and we admit that we do not succeed very well. We realize that the gap between what we might know and what we actually do know keeps growing, because the knowledge made available to human beings by the sciences is growing much faster than what an individual can assimilate. We admit that we should practice justice and charity in our relations with others, yet at the same time we are aware of a pervasive and virulent selfishness. We cannot get rid of our metaphysical need, our groping awareness of God. Yet we feel inclined to resist God, preferring to stay on earth, the earth we investigate and use with our own power, to our own profit. We want to realize ourselves (as the saying goes) and yet we keep failing. Our life goals remain unrealized. We set up high standards for our environment and society; we fight for a more ideal organization of our society. And the new organization is as much a disappointment as the former one. It is ephemeral, premature, dragging along the unforeseen consequences of what we had in mind. There is no need to go on with a description of this dualism between utopia and reality. We all know of it, suffer from it in our own lives, and in our dealings with Church and State.

THE IDEALISTIC AND THE REALISTIC SOLUTION
OF THE CONFLICT

Equally well known are the many false ways that are used to take care of this basic human situation. A brief mention of them will suffice.

First there are the idealists who cannot get along with reality and try to escape into the heaven of their ideals. Countless are the ways and methods of such false idealism that we, sinners that we are, all practice to some extent. Here is the person who wants to get out of public life, who is unwilling to dirty his hands with politics, who is looking for a quiet realm of private happiness, of leisure, of mere estheticism, of pure ideas. There are the snobs, the homesick, the romantics, the people whose slogan is Horace's *"Odi profanum vulgus et arceo"* (I hate the vulgar mob and I keep it away from me). There are the Christian idealists whose main occupation is to suffer on account of their Church. There is the person who regrets the greatness and splendor of the former German Reich. There are those who have fathomed the shabbiness and wretchedness of their fellow human beings (generally not their own; however, when they have unmasked themselves, they enjoy this too as the most sublime form of idealism and truth). All these and many other forms of idealism have this in common: that they consider what they discover in human reality, explicitly or implicitly in human conduct, as *hopelessly* and pitifully wanting. Idealists in this sense are basically people whose "ideals" are not contained in reality, even in germ, but merely hover above so-called reality as its condemnation. This attitude, as we said, does not have to take shape in a theory. It is present where one can only suffer from reality; where one tries to keep away from everything painful, like cardiac patients who avoid whatever might upset them; where one finds in one's beloved ideals solace for failures in real life; where one looks instinctively for protection from present social crises, there to remain as unbothered as possible; where one knows everything better than others, especially politicians and church leaders, who are responsible for the lamentable everyday reality.

The second way in which one wrongly tries to tackle the basic human condition and its dualism is that of the so-called realists. They are proud of the sober outlook with which they view the shabbiness of life and of humanity, without getting upset about it.

They are ethical Darwinists, who take it for granted that human life is a struggle for existence in which the hardiest come out on top. They coldly consider the utterances of politicians and clergy to be unrealistic fog, which others — but not they themselves — need as analgesic for life's woes. They hold on to the solid pleasures of life, while carefully avoiding excess. If they still think occasionally of God, they consider their success in life a concrete proof of the divine blessings they deserve. They are fierce and convinced defenders of the social order as the best protector of their own profitable situation. We might add, of course, that there are such closet realists in the Church.

FRAGMENTS OF A CHRISTIAN ANSWER

Keeping in mind this dualism, which is ineradicably rooted in human nature, and the false attitudes, made possible although not justified by this dualism, a few things are to be said about the Christian way of shaping life and the world between the ideal and the real. Let it be said at once that we can, of course, not give practical prescriptions, and that whatever can be said is presented here in rather arbitrarily selected fragments. We are not offering advice for a specific purpose, for which concrete directions should be given. We are speaking in general about self-realization and self-understanding, which cannot be put down in something like a system of coordinates, from a position outside of them. If therefore appeal has to be made to our all-encompassing existence, which loses itself in God's incomprehensibility, it stands to reason that this appeal can be made only in rather arbitrarily chosen fragments.

TAKING THE UTOPIA OF GOD SERIOUSLY

It is possible to define the Christian understanding of existence as the conviction that what seems to be utopian is the true reality. Hence so-called reality must be viewed as utterly dependent, as provisional, as that which possesses the lower degree of reality, even though we should not, like some Eastern mystics, consider it a mere unreal appearance. This in fact is obvious or, rather, should gradually become obvious through the experience of a long

Christian life. Do we not say: There exists an infinite, absolute, eternal God, who is distinct from the world and for whom we are intended; the history of our freedom terminates inexorably in the very immediacy of this God, whom we hope to meet as our redeeming, forgiving, liberating judgment. At the same time, however, Christian faith does not overlook the fact that this God dwells in inaccessible light, that even in face to face vision, God remains for all eternity unfathomable in his nature and in the decisions of his freedom. That is precisely why Christian faith exhorts us to take seriously the world and our tasks in it, with all their humdrum, apparently ephemeral trifles. Our faith tells us that we are responsible before God for this world and our tasks in it, insofar as they depend on the freedom with which we are entrusted. As St. Paul says, this is the way we must work out our salvation: in fear and trembling. For our innermost existence in freedom, as it is inexorably imposed upon us, God is not just a random or even doubtful factor at the edge of our existence, one we might discreetly and somewhat skeptically ignore. God is the reality that suffuses everything, orders everything, attracts everything toward himself and away from us. And precisely as this incomprehensible reality, God renders all other realities around us questionable, relative, and imbued with their own incomprehensibility.

Are we Christians not the people who call this utopia, which we cannot control either in thought or in action, God, whom we consider the true and genuine reality? Are we Christians not the people who consider heaven not only an additional boon that one might (and why not?) welcome at the end but as an integral part of our earthly reckoning and of our "real" life? Of course, one should proclaim a Gospel that loves the earth. Of course, it is impossible to take the tasks of this earth, if correctly understood, seriously enough; of course, one should praise the beauty of the earth, the greatness of humanity, the splendor of love. But it remains true that the God for whom we are headed, for whom we exist, to whom we will have to render an account, is totally other, totally different from the "real" realities with which our experience is concerned. And this God may not be reduced to being the mere splendor with which we exalt our own reality, or try at least to render it somewhat more cheerful. As Christians we are deeply convinced that we exist for God. In his sovereign absolute majesty God is not just an additional item that must balance the budget of our life. Only when we have decided to adore God in his absolute sovereignty, only when we even try to love God with a boldness that seems to be wholly beyond our power, only when in awed silence we capitulate before his incomprehensibility and welcome this capitulation of our knowledge and our life as the beginning of our deepest freedom and our eternal salvation, only then do we start to be Christians. Are we then not the people of a holy utopia and not the people of a so-called realism? Are we not convinced that by thinking and living in this way we grasp genuine reality, whereas we consider and treat what we call reality as merely a stage, something provisional, even something that is secretly already suffused with and saved by the so-called utopia.

And so the theme of Christian existence between utopia and reality confronts us with the inexorable question: Are we successful in our attempts to consider and to treat as the genuine reality a remote utopia which seems at first very unreal, very difficult to measure and hard to handle, compared to which the obvious solid reality becomes unreal? Do we Christians have the courage to reverse the standards with which we measure what we consider to be the real? Do we have the courage to feel that we are, as the Bible says, pilgrims and aliens in a world that allows one to speak of God at most only at the graveside or from the pulpit, and that finds it embarrassing to talk about God anywhere else? Is all of this too weighty for the idealist, too utopian for the realist? Are God and faith in eternal life part of our everyday life, or is this reality only an object of pious devotion on Sundays, whereas our everyday morality does not really differ from that of an atheist? Let there be no doubt about it: The "between" of the duality "utopia and reality" truly means that we must turn upside down the standards with which we judge reality and that the appeal of the so-called utopia should be for us the most solid reality.

ENDURING THE LASTING TENSION
BETWEEN FULFILLMENT AND LACK OF IT

What all of this really means for us becomes clear when we keep in mind that this tension between utopia and reality, the ideal and the real, is not accepted as soon as we affirm a theoretical statement about it. What is ultimately at stake is not that we Christians affirm *theoretically* the lasting tension between the ideal and the real, between heaven and earth. Accepting such a theoretical statement is not the same as reacting in the right way to this tension. Theoretically one can be a Christian and still unconsciously in practical life, by siding either with idealism or with so-called realism, not live up to this tension that confronts our freedom. As long as the history of our freedom has not reached its goal, we are always *in via*, always pilgrims, and thus always people who disrupt to some extent the unity in diversity that is given with this tension. We are people who half-heartedly avoid the radical appeal that is called God, who overlook the fact that we must always correspond to this absolute appeal by faithfully fulfilling our earthly tasks. We are told that we must love God with our whole heart and our whole strength, and, at the same time, admit that we are sinners. Does this not imply that we never totally answer God's absolute appeal, that like idealists we do not take the familiar reality of our existence seriously enough as the way of obeying God's appeal, or that we do it in the wrong way by claiming, like the realists, that daily duty has nothing to do with God's absolute appeal. We are in fact, all of us, half-hearted, unable to discover the right stance between that appeal and so-called reality. We are always swinging back and forth between the danger of losing our hearts to an idealistic dreamlike heaven and the danger of godlessly loving the earth. Moreover, the Christian message teaches that we cannot even tell ourselves with conscious certitude *exactly which* position we occupy within this tension. We are invited to be full of hope and leave to God's judgment the question of how things really stand with us, of whether we have a good or a bad conscience. We come from a beginning that we ourselves did not initiate. We plod along like pilgrims on a road whose end disappears in the incomprehensibility and the freedom of God; we are stretched between heaven and earth, and we have neither the right nor the possibility of giving up either one. One is not the other, yet neither can be realized without the other. We never know with absolute certitude how our deepest freedom stands with regard to this unavoidable situation of our existence; we have to accept our origin, and we must give our deepest love to the appeal and the end that are called God. And whether or not we really do this, even that we must hopefully leave to God. Christian existence cannot forego any of these requirements. That constitutes its greatness, its radical difficulty, and its ultimate obviousness, because outside of it there is nothing that it might question.

LIVING WITH HOPE IN GOD

To accept in the right and salutary way the unavoidable dualism between the ideal and the so-called real is called in usual Christian terminology "hope borne by God's grace." Hope is one of the three basic attitudes that establish humanity in a right relationship to God. It is obvious that the salutary acceptance of the enduring tension between the ideal and the so-called real can be called Christian hope. Christians cannot decide for themselves what their "ideal" is to be. Rather they are obliged to strive for the absolute reality of God in immediacy. If they did not do this they would miss the essential destiny that they cannot refuse. Christians have no right to be satisfied with a fulfillment that would be less than God in himself. They have no right to settle down forever in their own finiteness, which would remain familiar and could be arranged as they please. They have to make God their hope, their absolute hope. The eternally incomprehensible God cannot be put, with his essence and his freedom, into a system of coordinates that would be more comprehensive than God. That is why this hopeful striving for God necessarily appears to be totally beyond our power. It can be endured only because God, through his own reality, renders us able to endure it. In that sense we have a right to say that Christian hope is a utopia, since God alone, whom we can neither grasp nor manipulate, allows us to demonstrate that it is possible and meaningful.

Accepting a permanent dualism between the ideal and the real is, when interpreted in a Christian way, really utopian, not only because of the end for which our hope strives but also because of the starting point of this striving. The dualism which we have to endure between the ideal and the so-called real asks us to strive for God, who is not one available object among the so-called realities with which we deal in our daily activities. This hope that aims beyond everything graspable is not supposed to leave the so-called realities behind in their empty glitter; it must carry them along in this hopeful movement, bringing them to perfection as a mediation of its own irresistible dynamism toward God, without identifying God with this mediation. The so-called realities remain different, provisional, impossible to harmonize, yet precisely because we endure and accept them in their limitation, conditionality, and contradiction, they make it possible for us really to accept God as the only absolute goal to our hope and striving. We hope in God when we accept the earthly realities in fidelity as provisional, perishable, and fragile, without trying to find in them a definite end. Hope keeps on advancing and always carries along with itself, while mysteriously transforming, the things which it seems patiently to skip.

PATIENTLY WAITING FOR THE DAWNING OF GOD'S MYSTERY AMID THE GROWING PERPLEXITY

But as we try in this way patiently to accept the immediate so-called realities as mediation of our absolute hope, this so-called reality remains nonetheless what it is and as it is imposed upon us: incomprehensible, forever unfinished, forever resisting a harmonious synthesis. All of this is getting worse today in a way that could not have been imagined in former times. While more and more of reality falls within human powers, at the same time it remains as incomprehensible and unfinished as ever. These features affect our own activity and freedom; they are turning into a burden that humankind has never before experienced to this extent. Let us honestly admit it: Our bewilderment keeps growing. True, we are forced, individually and collectively, to make decisions, an obligation we cannot shirk. But the presuppositions of these decisions are becoming less and less transparent. The more the natural and human sciences develop, continually providing more data for consideration before any major decision, the less transparent are the conditions for our decision. So many possibilities and points of view are presented that we get lost. Today only the simpleminded and the foolish know exactly what should be done by individuals and groups. In earlier times, it seemed as though nature,without consulting us, had imposed on us or pre-programmed for our decision most of what made up our life. That is why more things were obvious to us than is the case today. Individually and collectively, painfully groping and half-blind, we advance along life's path.

To accept such perplexity, to admit and bear it, belongs to our Christian task. We must today carry it out soberly and without idealistic obfuscation. For Christians, perplexity in life is, in the final analysis, nothing but the concrete dawning of the sacred mystery that we call God. Our perplexity should ultimately not astonish us. Wherever we can, we should get rid of it, try to clear it up. But even if we fight it bravely and resolutely, we will not overcome it. It lingers, it overpowers individuals in their lives. The only question is whether we take it as the unveiling of the basic absurdity of life *or* as the concrete dawning of the Mystery that we accept as our saving, forgiving, fulfilling, and absolute future. This is ultimately the only alternative, from which we cannot run away.

However, the option for either alternative can once more become strangely veiled and ambiguous. An attitude that pretends to be a quiet hope of eternal life may in reality be the veil hiding a so-called realistic way of life that is satisfied in false moderation with the scanty happiness of the present life. And the passionate, seemingly desperate protest against the absurdity of our existence may be the way in which a fundamental hope may be realized, a hope that finds what it is looking for nowhere on earth, a hope for infinite fulfillment.

Although we may still hear the last echoes of a triumphant humanism that claims to have reached the limits of its self-made fulfillment, today we are assailed by a feeling that we have lost our way, a feeling that all our beautiful ideals are quickly becoming threadbare. Dissonant voices urge us to do a thousand things at once; hopelessness is spreading so inexorably that all ideals, old and new, all programs for the future, which still have a following, look pitiful and lack impact.

In this situation we Christians are not allowed to give up, we must continue to do what our times and every-day life expect from us. We do not even have the right to hope for an end to earthly progress in our history and society. We Christians know that ultimately we should not and cannot choose at our liking the time for the history of our salvation. That is why as human beings and as Christians we have no reason to pretend to be very cheerful nowadays. It seems to me that, if we are honest, we must say that we are living in a wintry season, wintry in both society and Church. Undoubtedly we always have good reasons to demand more from ourselves than we can actually accomplish. But we do not have to ask too much from ourselves, nor from politicians, nor from church leaders. We do not have to act as if, with a little more courage and good will, our individual and collective situation would be changed into one of sheer pleasure and joy. Demanding too much would show that we are putting our hope not in God, but in ourselves.

If the global situation that we are living through, which looks like a harsh winter, is imposed on us, then, having done what we are able with resignation and patience, we have the right to accept the situation as the mysterious dawning of the eternal mystery of God, the end we can and must reach. Christians should not try to avoid failure, disappointment, and adversity by means of strange ideological nostrums that are for sale in society and in the Church. They can, with faith, hope, and charity, accept these adversities as the nearing of the incomprehensible God. The more frightful, the more hopeless everything looks, the more certain is God's arrival.

THE TEST OF DEATH

What we have said must now be put somewhat more concretely, even at the risk of sounding pietistic, of smacking of that private interiority that can be defended today only by an old-fashioned theology. Each of us has to answer before God questions of whether we have fulfilled our political task, whether we have loved our neighbor, whether we have respected people's freedom and treated them with justice. If this life of ours, with its unavoidable "political" component, has been lived the right way, it will be gloriously harvested in our eternity. Yet it moves inexorably toward death, which does not carry us away into nothingness, but forever surrenders us with the history of our freedom. Our death must be endured by us in loneliness before God. And that is where it will be revealed to each of us once and for all whether we have faced in our life the tension between the ideal and the so-called real; whether we have run away from that tension, either into a pseudo-idealism or a pseudo-realism; whether we have always renewed our efforts to overcome the tension between the ideal and the real, aiming at the point where our contribution might be tendered, where we ourselves, having been enabled by God's grace fully to realize our ideal, will have been united in blessed union with the eternal God in his infinite, holy, incomprehensible splendor.

4

THE THEOLOGICAL DIMENSION
OF PEACE

Peace is a very complex reality. That is why the topic of peace has many aspects to it. I would like to say a few words here about a theological dimension of peace. Peace has in fact many theological dimensions, for all the complex realities that make for peace in the family, in the neighborhood, in the state, in the international community of peoples, refer, each one in its own way, to God; hence the many aspects of the theological dimension of peace. But I intend to shed some light only on one of these dimension, without touching the others.

Let us, for brevity's sake, call "conflict" the opposite of peace. We may then inquire: How does conflict arise? The answer is that conflict among people presupposes that the many realities, particularities, and dimensions that make up humankind, the human community, and its environment do not from the start harmonize without friction. No wonder, since in this world created by God created, hence finite, realities do not constitute a harmony in which every reality immediately fits in with all others. Possibly there are explanations for this beyond the fact that the world and whatever is in it are finite and borne by history. At any rate, this is the way things are, and we have simply to accept this fact humbly and soberly. The multifarious realities do not — at least to the human mind — fit together harmoniously.

REASONABLE ADJUSTMENTS AND COMPROMISES

As a result of this situation conflict arises among people because they disagree about the way of fitting together the various components of human existence. Every person defends, so to speak, the particular nature of a certain reality, and is unwilling to yield anything on behalf of another element within human existence, which in turn makes its own claims. There is, for instance, only a limited amount of wealth. Everyone lays claim to a greater part of it. Total harmony must be brought about at the cost of some sacrifices to be made by the individual components. When people cannot agree where and from whom such sacrifices, such restrictions, such concessions should be demanded, conflict arises among them.

Now it is clear that almost every such conflict might be settled with the help of some common sense, moderation, and peaceableness. We only have to find out where and to what extent certain concessions can be imposed so as to reach some balance among the various claims of the different realities. We might say that, roughly speaking, all conflicts can be settled. Peace can be reached in the various personal and social domains if everyone is willing to accept such reasonable and obvious restrictions, sacrifices, and concessions. Basically all efforts to reach peace aim at an equilibrium between the claims of individuals and those of groups. As a rule, resolution of conflict is brought about by reasonable adjustments and compromises.

THE REALM OF UNCONDITIONED FREEDOM

Yet, on closer examination, there are in human life many cases of conflicts and endeavors to settle them where things are not so simple. For in many instances — possibly in all conflicts of some importance — it happens that one of the parties in such a conflict may be forced to forego something for the sake of peace and yet receive no perceptible compensation in return. True, very often we cay say that a compromise that leads to peace is better for all parties than if one party tries to prevail, without foregoing its own wishes or needs. In a trade war or in a modern nuclear war all parties would fare worse than if they are agreed on a reasonable compromise whereby each one of them would have given up some advantages.

Yet, as we said above, in many cases at least, or maybe even in all serious conflicts, there are situations in which peace is possible only if either or both parties forego something without any compensation, or even without a word of thanks from the other side, as if the outcome were obvious. How would the woman who in midlife has been hurt by the infidelity of her husband be rewarded if, for the sake of the children, she foregoes a divorce? What about a politician who in a political conflict respects the truth and, in order to stay honest, admits that he was wrong, showing that he has regard for the rights of his opponent as much as for his own? Do people respect and thank him for it? Or is he not publicly or privately mocked as an idiot who cannot take care of himself? There are in human life then situations in which concessions and sacrifices are expected that are not really and manifestly rewarded in a sufficient and visible way by the peace that ensures. Life's accounts, even with regard to peace, never come out exactly and smoothly through nicely balanced human computations.

This is the area where a religious dimension of peace comes up, of which we intend to say a few words. In the final analysis, if we do not want to destroy ourselves, we cannot simply give up all claims to things that are radically important for our own existence and self-realization, or that are generally considered such, without demanding that this sacrifice be compensated in some other way. But how will this sacrifice be compensated, when such a compensation is obviously impossible in ordinary experience? There are enough conflicts in which we wonder bitterly, and not without reason, why we ourselves should be the "sucker" who has to pay so that there may be peace.

In such cases persons can have the generosity and inner freedom to accept such sacrifices in silence and without reward only if they are open to that reality and fulfillment which we call God. We might almost say by way of definition: God is the real, universal, and all-encompassing possibility of that peace, the possibility and meaningfulness of which can no longer be shown by means of the individual elements that constitute human reality. In the final analysis only those persons can be peace-loving who are convinced that there is a being able to bestow upon human existence an ultimate, undeniable, indestructible meaningfulness. We call that being God.

Those who believe in God feel no need frantically to defend as absolute something that is so meaningful to them that, even in a radical human conflict, they would be unwilling to give it up. Only those persons who are open to God and to their own fulfillment in God do not have to accept an all-out conflict, when they are faced with the need of sacrifice for the sake of peace, even a sacrifice that takes away from them important values. That is why the question of the presuppositions of peace points to a religious dimension. Persons who, for the sake of peace, succeed in renouncing very important values without thanks or approbation, and even at times without being rewarded by the feeling of their own unselfishness, only such persons have, whether they know it or not, reached the realm of unconditional peace, the realm of the grace of God.

NOT PUTTING UP WITH EVERYTHING

We have referred to God as the condition of the possibility of peace through a renunciation that is not rewarded by some other advantage. This does not mean, of course, that every conflict can be settled in this way. There have always been powerful rulers who, for the sake of a peace that suits them well, urge others to give in, to be quiet and reasonable. Such rulers selfishly want to turn religion into the opium of the people. To reach their own purposes they exhort others to be submissive, reasonable, willing to make sacrifices, and to yield without protest. Persons who are totally open to God and who discover in God the ultimate unsurpassable justification of their way of acting may also in some instances resist, fight, and incur the risk of war, even though they cannot be certain of a favorable outcome. Those who have God for an ally do not have to put up with everything; when their conduct is lawful in God's eyes, they cannot perish in such a conflict.

What we should do in individual cases, whether we should fight for the sake of legitimate earthly realities or, prompted by God, make some sacrifice for the sake of peace, cannot be decided in the light of such general considerations. Persons who are free in God may, in some instances, either venture into conflict or avoid it, and they may do this on the ground of the same ultimate relation to God. In the domain of everyday experience, there exists a love of peace that goes without reward and that people can harbor only if they are open to God. Naturally this also implies that such peace-loving people are open to God, even if they cannot explicitly tell themselves that they are.

5

THE PROBLEM OF
EUROPE'S FUTURE

I shall start with a few preliminary remarks that may, perhaps somewhat immodestly, be called part of a philosophy and theology of history. It is, of course, impossible in an article of this length to offer a philosophy and theology of history with all their many and different themes. Nor may we take for granted that they are known and apply them to our problem of Europe's future. The only thing we can do is choose, perhaps somewhat arbitrarily, a few considerations from this philosophy and theology. Explaining them rather than starting from an empirical analysis of the present situation may show more clearly why we have a right to inquire about Europe's future. Let me present some considerations without explicitly distinguishing between a *philosophy* and a *theology* of history.

THE FUTURE AND THE PROBLEM OF THE WHOLE

Mere historical curiosity naturally gives thought not only to the present but also to the possibilities of the future. Positivistic pragmatism, after the manner of politicians and futurologists, probes the foreseeable future of the world as well as of Europe. The question we are about to examine might for a start be formulated as follows: Are there other reasons and considerations showing that it is meaningful and necessary to inquire about Europe's future?

Today's sceptics understand rather easily that such an inquiry does not immediately make sense. It is true that Europe refers to a certain region distinct from other parts of the world. Its history too has some unity that separates it from other historical developments. With all its diversity it shows some "cultural" unity that distinguishes it from other cultures. It possesses a common biological (ethnic) substratum; it has its European community, and so on. Nevertheless, one might wonder whether the word "Europe" does not signify an object that, on closer examination, disintegrates before the observer into the destinies of individuals or into a network of causes and effects that, despite all artificial delimitations, is, or is slowly becoming, identical with the totality of human history.

Today's sceptics will further inquire whether it is possible to make any even slightly reliable predictions about the real future of Europe and of the world. Is it not a fact that, except for the very near future and for foreseeable developments, especially of a technical nature, we know and can know, nothing about the future?

Today's sceptics will ask whether it is possible to say anything serious about the "meaning" of the future of humanity in general and of Europe in particular. They have the impression that one can discover *particular* connections between aspects of their history and their society, which may at times mean something like real progress. But such particular findings, like small islands of meaning in an ocean of the unknown and the unknowable, do not yield any clear meaning of the whole. Nor do they yield any norms that tell us how things *ought* to go further, either for the "meaning" of the history of humankind as a whole or for Europe in particular.

Finally, today's sceptics will admit a few moral norms for their private lives and their immediate environment, but they will be inclined to doubt whether it is possible to enunciate binding moral norms for history and politics in general. Determining factors in biology and economics may allow some predictions, but it is doubtful whether norms, ideals, and directions can be formulated for the way in which Europe itself should envisage its own future. Even if we overlook the skeptical experiences of the present, the problem of Europe's future seems to be a very obscure problem.

It is not a particular or a "regional" problem within the totality of individuals and their world. It concerns the totality itself. That is why (although it needs the help of particular sciences and human experience) it is ultimately a problem of metaphysics, of faith, of an option that can supply an answer only to those who fully trust this special kind of knowledge, in which persons are involved as a whole with the whole of their reality. All these decisions about the future of Europe directly or indirectly concern the *entire* person amid the peoples of Europe as a whole and, given the present unity of world history, the totality of humankind. Such questions are ultimately no longer questions about this or that fragment in the whole of reality. They are questions about the whole world. That is also why such questions can be asked and answered only as a result of a precomprehension of the whole of reality. They are, as it were, not questions about a single point *in* a system of coordinates but questions *about* the system itself as a whole — and thus questions of a metaphysical anthropology and of the way persons understand themselves in faith. Moreover, they are questions that cannot be answered only through an abstract theory. In order to be answered "rationally" and in a responsible way, they require a free decision, faith, and the help of praxis. One would misunderstand human existence if one were to think that ultimate clarity and certainty can be reached by abstract knowledge alone, independently of an existential option.

ABOUT THE REALITY OF EUROPE

We are now trying to reflect on the different elements of our problem and to do it in the manner mentioned above, which, compared with the historical sciences and with an empirical analysis of the present time is somewhat a priori.

Here is our first question: Can we take it for granted that Europe is a "reality" about whose present and future state we can seriously say anything really important? The question itself is not very clear and should first be explained. When Christian metaphysicians and theologians say something about individual persons, they are convinced (or at least were until the Enlightenment) that these persons have a lasting and definitive value in their nature and in the history of their freedom, that they are "immortal," that, with the enduring achievements of their history and despite all necessary transformations, they end up forever in the eternity of God. This continues to be the conviction of Christians, at least on the basis of their faith. In this sense persons, at least as individuals, have absolute significance, absolute importance. They cannot be reduced to disparate elements and thus be eliminated.

Hence, as a Christian metaphysician and theologian, one can inquire whether such absolute significance and importance also belongs to human collectivities, or whether such units (a social group, a people, a historical epoch, a culture, and so on) belong only to those unavoidable but purely provisional phenomena within whose ephemeral reality persons must develop the history of their own freedom, mere phenomena that disappear as soon as the proper meaning and achievement of history have been reached in the definitiveness of each persons before God. When one seriously considers the possibility that human collectivities may have, at least analogically, such absolute significance as, according to our Christian faith, belongs to human persons, one may also be emboldened to inquire whether "Europe" belongs to the collectivities that are endowed with eternal significance. This does not mean, of course, that Europe will certainly exist *in time* as long as humankind as a whole exists. It means that Europe as such enters into the definitiveness of history, as does each human being, despite the brevity of human life.

Inquiring about the significance of collective human reality in general, and eventually of Europe in particular, may seem to people, in the humdrum of their everyday lives, like a meaningless and empty speculation. But when historical decisions have to be made for such a collectivity, in this instance for Europe, is it not of the greatest importance to know whether they are being made in the perspective of such an absolute meaning, rather than with the implicit, politically fashionable, rhetorically touted conviction that at the end everything turns to nought or, at most, retains some importance only in the fate of individuals? One may ignore this question as unrealistic and artificial. But a Christian remains convinced that politicians as persons are responsible for their decisions before the tribunal of God. And thus we may wonder whether they do not have to submit to God's judgment not only the "intention" that motivated their political decisions but also the real consequences of those decisions in history. Are there then collectivities that have a significance which stands somehow (difficult to determine, of course) on the same level as that of individual subjects, although that significance is naturally not quite the same? If the answer to this question is affirmative, one may further inquire whether this may also apply to the collectivity "Europe," since it stands to reason that all collectivities do not have the same importance.

THE SIGNIFICANCE OF COLLECTIVE REALITIES

It is clear that this question can be answered only in connection with a human existential ontology. We can touch on it only briefly here. In the history of anthropology a perennial conflict exists between two conceptions of humanity. According to the first, persons are, in the final analysis, absolute individuals, free subjects, who ultimately exist in radical loneliness. All their "social" dimensions, starting from their biological dependence and extending to the most exalted and sublime creations of their social life, may be understood only as subordinate conditions that make it possible for them to be truly unique persons in freedom. According to the second conception, individuals are not only in fact members of a collectivity, they also exist and can be understood *only as such*. Individuals exist only so that the collectivity may exist, whatever the nature of this collectivity. Human individuality and human sociality probably represent (I do not want to put it more strongly) two ontological determinations of the human. They cannot exist independently of one another. Neither can one be reduced to the other as a mere aspect of it, as a condition of its possibility, and so on. These are two fundamental determinations of humanity, whose unity and difference are given simultaneously. In both this difference in unity and this unity in difference they refer to the mystery of the one God. It is in God's transcendent unity that the possibility of unity in diversity is rooted, in such a way that the different realities cannot be reduced to each other, while nevertheless constituting a real unity. (It stands to reason that this dialectic of unity and diversity, which finite realities cannot surmount, must be understood in many different ways, according to the degree of being and the multiple composition of each one of them.)

Let us suppose then (we might almost say with metaphysical boldness) that individuality and sociality are determinations of one and the same person that originate together and cannot be adequately reduced to each other. It follows then that, if persons have an absolute and eternal importance and significance, the same characteristics must also be ascribed to their sociality. Consequently, human collectivities too have an analogous (although different) importance and definitiveness before God, similar to the one which a solid anthropology and Christian faith attribute to the person as an individual subject of freedom.

From the point of view of the history of Christian faith as well, the significance of collective human realities is almost obvious. In the history of salvation and faith (of both the Old and the New Testament) an almost frightful development has occurred. Christian faith can assimilate it only by presupposing that the convictions that explicitly succeed each other in this history constitute the totality of the Christian understanding of humanity only if they are taken together, and that the stages of this history do not obliterate each other. In the Old Testament God made a covenant with a people, not strictly speaking with individuals. It does not matter here whether God, in privileging this partner Israel among a multitude of peoples, has chosen *only* that people, or whether an analogous relation of God to all other peoples cannot also be accepted. Such a relation would then have been more explicitly grasped by Israel; it became the foundation of the existence of Israel as a people. At any rate, here a *people* is the addressee of the divine activity. Individuals are important only if and insofar as they take part in the righteous activity of this people, as directed by its covenant with God. Individuals (in their explicit conscious mind) feel safe and know that they are approved and accepted by God if this people continues to live in an obedient relationship to the God of the covenant. The least we can say is that, through long centuries of Israel's history of faith, the question of the eternal significance of the individual is less important than the significance of the people before God.

In the New Testament, after a *pre*-history of the specifically Christian anthropology that still belongs to the history of Israel, the way humankind is considered undergoes a change. It is true that we still hear of the Christian message being announced to peoples. Other similar Old Testament allusions to collectivities do not simply disappear, especially since the Church, as the main source of salvation, is herself a collectivity. Yet individuals and their salvation are now clearly occupying the foreground. Each one decides in freedom about his or her salvation and will with an inalienable responsibility, stand as an individual before the judgment seat of God.

We should not say that these two conceptions are mutually exclusive, and that a New Testament "individualism" (if we can call it that) is the only valid position to be seriously considered in a Christian interpretation of history. Old Testament theology *also* remains valid. It recognizes "peoples" as subjects of salvation history, as it occurs within profane history. It speaks of their angels, God's name is invoked over them, a God of all *peoples*. To these peoples the Gospel of Jesus is preached. Hence it is difficult simply to reduce the salvation history of these peoples (hence their profane history as well) to that of individuals, even as the profane history of peoples cannot be reduced to the mere random interaction of individual histories. They undoubtedly influence each other, but together they also constitute a single meaningful whole. We Christians speak of God's eternal Reign, of the eternal communion of the saints with God. If we do not want to imagine, in the definitiveness of history in God, a kind of hierarchical grouping of individuals organized merely according to a formally moral standard, then, in this eternal realm of the definitiveness of freedom, the individuality of the supraindividual collective histories of peoples should also be maintained and recognized. *How* the diverse histories of such collectivities can enter into the definitive realm of freedom is beyond our present powers of comprehension, but it should be possible if history is not to have an ephemeral meaning but is itself to reach God's definitiveness. It should be possible if its contribution is to be more than some colorless production of morality or a mere sum of isolated free subjects who do not take with them into the definitiveness of history their collective historical unity. So we may boldly claim that historical collectivities also enter as such into the final consummation of history. They are more than ephemeral realities.

EUROPE AS PART OF
THE DEFINITIVE CONSUMMATION OF HISTORY

At this point the question arises whether Europe belongs to these realities to which one may attribute an absolute eternal significance, so that the problem of its future would derive its ultimate right and importance from that eternal significance.

First let us say that a positive answer to this question does not imply that Europe as a historical entity and not just as a geographical reality must remain forever ("until the end of time") a notable historical reality. True, on the authority of the letter to the Romans, traditional Christian doctrine ascribes to the people of Israel as a historical reality a duration until the end of human history. We do not have to consider the question whether this idea is a dogma of the Christian theology of history or only a plausible idea. For people of earlier times, realities that were spatially, and even more temporally, very small and limited made up the history of humankind. People thought that history would not last very long, thus they could easily imagine that a single people might endure until the end of time, even while they were witnessing the downfall of whole peoples. Still, the thesis of the eternal significance of Europe before God does not imply the conviction that Europe as a historical collectivity has to be historically important forever to an extent that is in some way comparable to its importance today beyond its spatial reality. Even if Europe in that sense should "vanish" from the history of humankind, like other peoples that have disappeared, it might nevertheless belong to those historical realities that remain significant before God in and through the definitive salvation of their members. Of course, our inquiry also implies the question why and how Europe, through the *content* of its history, could continue as a collective individuality that would remain forever significant in the definitive consummation of universal history. Clearly we cannot present a detailed discussion of this question here.

The historical significance of Europe within the total definitive meaning of history before God derives from two reasons: first, from the special nature and importance of its profane history in itself and for the whole of humankind, an importance that has significance "anonymously" for salvation history; next, from the special contribution made by Europe in the history of its faith and its explicit salvation history, a contribution that is peculiar to it, as compared with the faith and salvation history of other peoples, and in this way is important also for other peoples.

While trying to demonstrate the "eternal" significance and importance of Europe by means of its function and achievements in the history of salvation, we do not mean, of course, that this is the only reason we attribute to it such eternal significance. We mean only that this is the easiest way to show its importance. These achievements in the history of faith and salvation could concretely occur only in connection with the secular and temporal accomplishment of Europe. Moreover, many things happen in secular history that, through God's grace, are anonymously Christian. That is why the secular history of Europe and its peoples has eternal significance when we attribute to Europe a specific and unique task and achievement in the world's history of salvation and faith.

We do not have to consider the question of whether and how "Europe" should or should not be distinguished from the West, and how exactly its derivation from the history of Israel and from the Roman-Greek-Byzantine culture should be considered as part of its nature. These and similar questions cannot be explicitly discussed here.

Even though the concept "Europe" is not exactly unequivocal, we can say that in the unity and despite the diversity of its peoples, Europe is a reality that belongs to salvation history in a way that is analogous to the special position which the Christian theology of history ascribes to the people of Israel. We say analogous because we do not want to answer the question of how far this resemblance goes and yet how great the essential difference is, from the point of view of salvation history, between Israel and Europe. Neither do we have to examine here whether God's "covenant" with Israel is so unique in the salvation history of humankind, that the fact of being a "covenant people" should be denied to all other peoples, or whether the unique character of God's covenant with Israel means only *that* uniqueness with which God, in his goodness, speaks in an ever unique way to each people. We must also not forget to mention that the Christ of all peoples is descended, in that concrete uniqueness that belongs to every event in history, from the people of Israel and from no other people. But if, despite God's universal salvific will, which embraces every place and time, and by which God makes himself into the innermost entelechy and the ultimate end of the whole world, there exists a real *history* of salvation, then, Europe really has a function, with respect to the salvation of the whole world, resembling that of Israel.

The salvation of the world, starting from Israel, has proceeded throughout the whole of history since Christ from Europe. The importance of all peoples in universal history itself has a history, in which these peoples do not make their decisive contribution to universal history all at the same time. Thus it is not a disparagement or a belittling of the historical vocation of peoples in Asia and Africa to admit that, despite its reprehensible colonialism, Europe has had for all peoples a unique significance. We can say with John that all peoples are called to adore God everywhere in spirit and in truth. They do not have to do it only in Jerusalem. It remains true however that the salvation of the whole world, in its enfleshment and explicitness, has a history. It is also true that salvation has come and continues to come through Europe in historical, ecclesial, and verbal concreteness to other peoples, somewhat in the way in which salvation originated from Israel. This historical uniqueness of Europe within salvation history allows us to consider Europe as one of the peoples that are also of eschatological importance before God, as they must be found in a theology of history that is not one-sidedly individualistic. It stands to reason that Europe's importance in salvation history is of particular significance in universal history, and that this can be seen in profane history as well.

It is true, as we will presently emphasize, that the future of humankind is for us practically unknown. Therefore we cannot know what special contribution Europe and other peoples will yet make to the *future* common history of humanity. This is true because, in a philosophy of history, it remains quite impossible to explain the factual course of history in the past, the present, and the future in such a way that the several stages and contributions of single peoples become clear for the whole of history. Nevertheless, we can mention some specific contributions of Europe to universal history, contributions that were morally required and that may rightly be considered as "progress" in the history of humanity.

Europe has brought about the unification of the diverse histories of peoples and cultures which used to be divided up regionally to a great extent. This unification into a single history of humankind makes all people interdependent. In this way Europe has introduced into what has become a unified history many features that the whole of humankind has adopted. We mean not only rational-technical civilization but also higher human values in cultural and social life. But this topic belongs to the following sections. At any rate, Europe's function in salvation history, which presupposes and includes the secular, human contributions of Europe to the history of humanity, entails a reality and significance that does not depend on individual preferences. For a theology of history, Europe is, at the least, a reality and challenge.

GOD'S SALVIFIC WILL FOR EUROPE

Perhaps we can explain what we said above more precisely. If Europe has a function in and a significance for the salvation history of the whole of humankind, and to some extent for profane history as well, and if this function and significance are analogous to that of Israel, then we may say analogically of Europe what, with Paul, the Christian theology of history says of Israel: God's promises are irrevocable; they are never withdrawn. We have already said that this does not necessarily mean that Europe will constitute an important historical reality for all times. But it does mean that Europe has made a contribution to the definitive reality and meaning of universal history before God, a contribution that, in the final analysis, is undoubtedly *positive*. This is not readily obvious.

In a rational appraisal and in the light of a Christian conscience, when one thinks of all the historical absurdities and horrors that have filled Europe's history, it is not obvious that Europe has brought forth many positive results or that it deserves to be saved by God. We might make the same appraisal of the history of Israel, filled as it was with guilt and rebellion against God. Yet revelation tells us that, against almost all expectation, God pronounced a judgment on Israel that is definitively positive. Can we have the same hope for Europe? True, without being able to give theoretical reasons, Christians have the right to hope that the history of freedom *as a whole* will have a positive meaning. But this alone does not allow them to attribute positive value to particular historical realities and developments. If, on scriptural grounds, Christians can hold these convictions with regard to Israel, then, without venturing to prophesy about the world's future, they also have the right to the conviction that God harbors for Europe a salvific will that is active and irrevocable. Although this conviction is by no means indisputable, it seems that Christians can hold it.

This allows the European rightly to feel self-respect and a certain pride, which does not imply a boastful comparison with other peoples and cultures. Rather it allows the European to be convinced that Europe, through its influence on salvation history and therefore on profane history also, has had and still has a positive significance for universal history that matters before God. It also means that, although ignorant of the future of the world and of universal history, Europeans have no reason to lose heart.

EUROPE AS THE OUTCOME OF A FREE HISTORY

With the reality and significance that we have ascribed to it, Europe is not a mere matter of fact, but the outcome of the free history of real people, who have freely shaped this Europe in spite of all kinds of difficulties and obstacles. And thus the question necessarily arises how the freedom of those who are shaping Europe is related to Europe and its future. The following paragraphs offer a few considerations in response to this question, although they are perhaps no more than questions and guesses and merely an arbitrary selection from among such possible questions.

If Europe is the result of the freedom of former times, and if one may presuppose that the history of this freedom is not at an end, but that it goes on, then the problem of Europe's future is one that confronts the freedom and responsibility of the individuals who are shaping Europe today and who will shape it tomorrow.

About this freedom and responsibility for Europe, one must first say that Europe's future cannot be predicted with certainty. At first sight this statement is undoubtedly a platitude. Who would venture a precise and comprehensive answer to the question of how Europe will look in the year 2200? But we must add that a concrete prognosis, which would give one knowledge of what will happen in the future, is *in principle* impossible. Of course, there exists the science of futurology; research is being conducted that uses current data and the forces they contain to predict the future of the world and of Europe in particular. Presently we will have to say that such efforts to look into the future constitute a task that cannot be disregarded. But first we should emphasize that, despite all predictions and efforts to foretell it, of its very nature the future will always remain unknown. Much as concrete history in the present, past, and future is ultimately an inextricable unity of necessity and freedom, so every dimension of the human situation is also determined in part by human freedom. But this freedom is not only a carrying out of what is necessary and foreseeable. It always contains an element of creativity that, strictly speaking, cannot be deduced from what has gone before. It is a free choice, a decision.

It is, of course, not possible to demonstrate here that, despite all coercive and determining factors forever acting upon them, persons are free beings. Nor is it possible to explain further *where* and how *within* human existence freedom is concretely at work, how human reflection is unable to pinpoint it exactly, how that which is immediately given to reflection is always an inextricable synthesis of necessity and freedom, and how therefore it remains always possible to declare that this concrete event was determined. Yet we must hold on to the conviction that freedom is not merely a meta-empirical postulate behind an objective world of mere necessity, which would only conceal the subject's freedom, if such freedom exists at all. At least for the subjects who are facing history, who experience their own freedom and responsibility, it is something that always in some way becomes manifest in history itself.

Freedom is not merely the permanent moving factor of reason, praxis not merely that which follows from theory (and its defects). Freedom always creates the new and the unexpected. The many possibilities offered to freedom are not simply objective data, they become such only through the intervention of creative freedom. That is why history is always the merging of the unforeseeable and therefore a journey into an unknown future. Moreover, even if we were to consider history as the mere unrolling of necessary causal connections, ultimately the future would not be predictable. An all-encompassing and exact knowledge of the whole of reality, which would be presupposed for a clear prognosis, is beyond the reach of the human mind, since humanity is only part of the whole of reality. Finally, it is not clear to what extent some kind of indeterminism may be admitted within the subatomic domain.

UNPREDICTABILITY OF THE FUTURE

The journey into the future is therefore also a journey into the dark unpredictability of this future. A responsible activity cannot simply ignore this situation and, with shallow naïveté, content itself with the clear predictability of the immediate future. This uncertain situation means that human activity calls for certain 'virtues" without which this journey into a dark future cannot be made in a worthy and realistic manner. We should act courageously and take risks, we should decide to attempt more than the obvious, the tried, and the tested. Our "tutiorism" should be a tutiorism of taking risks, which never forgets that a healthy future, one that does not depend only on humans, can be reached only if we are ready to eschew a lazy conservatism, for which what is tried and tested is the supreme norm of activity.

The "principle of hope" — unlike a mere reliance on what is certain — belongs to the essence of a freedom that accepts risks. It belongs also to freedom as a journey into darkness when the future of Europe is at stake. Of course principle alone does not enable us to demonstrate which of the competing historical forces at work in Europe represents a program that is right and that promises Europe a healthy future. But all such competing elements in the concert of Europe should always be ready to answer the question whether they really have the courage to venture into a dark future, whether they have decided to let the future itself do what it has a right to do.

FUTUROLOGY

For those who are aware of their responsibility for Europe's future, that future is always, of its very nature, veiled in darkness; it can never be adequately foreseen by rational reflection and examination. This does not mean, of course, that prevision and planning for the future are not tasks that are unconditionally incumbent on people. They can and must plan for the future. Time and again they must ask: Where can we go from here and where should we go? These questions belong to the nature of persons as free subjects in history, and nowadays their answers are even more necessary and more widely possible. Futurology, in the strict sense of the word, such as is possible in our time, did not exist in earlier times; in fact it was not possible to any extent. Today, as free subjects, persons have entered a new stage. They have become responsible for themselves in a way and to an extent that did not exist in the past despite all the planning that occurred.

For today's futurology the whole world, in its great complexity and the mutual interaction of its parts, is open to careful scrutiny. Formerly people commanded a view of only a small section of the earth's total reality. For their philosophy and theology of history the whole of humankind was but a formal postulate, an "Idea." Today futurology can try to predict the probable size of the human race a hundred years from now. To some extent, it can also compute in advance the quantity of resources available for humankind's biological survival in the future. Unlike former times, when people stumbled upon new and greater resources only by chance, it can systematically organized the search for them. In these and many other ways the future of humanity is entrusted in an entirely new way to people themselves and their active planning.

Persons are not and never will be absolute creators of themselves. Their creativity always involves presuppositions that do not depend on themselves, and involves inner and outer limits of their activity. Nevertheless, today persons are, to an extent that was unthinkable in the past, their own planners and creators, even though the experience of the *limits* of this self-shaping are once more and in new ways becoming clearer and harder to bear. Futurology, by which persons can shape their future, implies a wholly new responsibility. Not only can they plan, they must plan. This rational and technical pre-planning of their material and social environment, and even of their own biological make-up, is for free human subjects a duty that they cannot reject in a nostalgic yearning for the past when everything was simpler and more obvious. All of this applies to those who are responsible for the future of Europe as well.

THE COURAGE TO RISK AND TO PLAN

It is not easy for the Europeans who know that they are responsible for Europe's future to fulfill simultaneously and harmoniously the two obligations that we have mentioned: on the one hand, the courage to incur the risk of a future that basically cannot be computed in advance but that has to be shaped in creative freedom; on the other hand, sober and rational planning. If both obligations are simultaneously required, then Europeans also have the duty to give serious thought to the diverse sources of information and the criteria for such a futurology. The future of Europe, which demands the coordination of both these attitudes and tasks, should be the work not of a single person or of a select few, but ultimately of all Europeans. This brings up the question (as it always did, but always in a new way) of how this collective free subject, composed of a multiplicity of individuals, can discover Europe's future.

The problem of the right composition of the collective agents to shape Europe's future cannot be decided by means of general abstract criteria, such as democratic equality of rights. Attention must be paid to the qualifications that will enable them to carry out their task. The ordinary way of conceiving the legitimacy of a democratic society and of a parliamentary regime may be based too simply and rather naively on the conviction that political decisions are ultimately not decisions of a creative freedom, but are merely the result of a synthesis of moral principles that are always and everywhere valid ("human rights" for example) together with the "necessities of the moment," which can be ascertained by means of scientific and demographic methods. Political decisions are, or certainly should be, partially of this kind, but they are also the real decisions of a collective freedom that always demands that those who make them are really capable of such decisions.

HISTORICAL AND FUTURE IDENTITY OF EUROPE IN A WORLDWIDE SOCIETY

The question of Europe's future is undoubtedly a question about a real future that must freely be shaped by standing the test of future historical situations. But of its very nature it is also the task of safeguarding the basic identity of Europe with its past history. Otherwise Europe would still have its former name and geographical localization, but it would no longer really be Europe.

This brings up a fundamental problem for the philosophy of history: Can we expect the values that have taken shape in Europe's past history to survive? Or will these values in their specifically European peculiarity unavoidably and inexorably disappear in the future, because that future belongs to a global civilization that is more or less the same all over the world? This problem does not refer to the survival of so-called cultural values and historical "moments" as remnants of former times. If Europe is not physically obliterated, to some extent they will continue to exist.

Nor are we trying to find out whether Europe will *in fact* keep its own specific cultural values. The question is rather whether it is at all conceivable that a given regional culture *can* simply hold on to its own specific cultural characteristics and values in the global civilization that already exists and promises to exist in the future. Of course, in such a future worldwide civilization all historical regions will be interdependent, in universal communication with each other, sharing rational and technical knowledge. In such an environment the specific characteristics and values of a given culture will no longer be the same as they once were. The question is whether they can still survive at all. Or does the universal history of humankind tend inexorably toward a point where peoples and individuals, though they differ from each other in the color of their skin and the place where they live, no longer differ in what formerly distinguished the great cultures from one another?

There is no doubt that today we are still far from such a radical cultural uniformity in a generalized way of life (American, Russian or Chinese?). Nor can we doubt that in all great national and other cultures the trend toward uniformity is still counteracted by a resolve to insert one's own culture into the future of humankind in such a way that, despite peaceful coexistence and cultural exchange, contributory cultures may each remain distinct. But the question is whether such efforts in the future can be only a nostalgically delaying factor in history, or whether such a resolve (of Europe in our case) to keep its cultural originality and to transmit it to the future development of the whole of humankind can be a meaningful task and a right and a duty. The question is whether the resolve to remain faithful to oneself and to one's former history and characteristic ways of being human, and to continue to exist in this way in the future, can be justified before the historical and political conscience of Europe. Once more, the question is not whether Europe has this resolve and to what extent it will be carried out in the future. The question is only whether here and now such a resolve, aiming at the future, really makes sense. That is not quite clear.

Cultures may perish, as has frequently happened in the past, even though heirs of such deceased cultures have always survived. Now, if such a cultural death is possible, the question may arise whether it would not be better and more courageous for a doomed culture to realize that death is not far away and to accept it with resignation, just as individuals are supposed to do for their own unavoidable death. It might well be that, in the case of a dying culture, only shallow and ignorant people would behave as if their history were still to have a real future, while wise and courageous people would consciously forego such a spectacle. That is how Benedict left dying Rome, became a hermit in Subiaco and, in this and in no other way, became the "patron saint" of the West.

On the other hand, Christians draw from their theology of history the conviction that in principle it is possible for some specific cultural values, which are not to be found everywhere and always, to survive into a future that remains open. Their faith firmly holds that despite its particular origin an explicit Christianity will continue forever, although they cannot foresee what importance it will possess in the future empirical history, as compared with other historical influences and realities, and how exactly this historically imperishable Christianity will look in times to come. For instance, Holy Scripture, which will forever remain the foundation of Christianity, will retain the characteristics of its historical origins and still remain important for the future. That is why Christians cannot doubt that not every given historical particularity must eventually perish simply because it originated in history. We have demonstrated this conviction through the theology of history. This does not mean that this conviction might not also be derived, in a philosophy of history, from a study of actual history. We only wanted to submit one reason for this conviction, which, for a Christian humanist, may well be the simplest and the strongest.

DOWNFALL OR FUTURE OF EUROPE?

As to maintaining Europe's identity in future history, European Christians must face, in principle and in theory, two possibilities since neither may be rejected a priori: Europe may disappear as an autonomous and distinct cultural reality, fading into a global civilization that will absorb it; or it may in all essential respects retain its identity. The question is which of these abstract possibilities will be the one to be taken into account in making historical decisions. One will probably have to say that pondering this historical problem will, at present, not lead to a clear and unequivocal answer, so that Europe's future still remains uncertain for us. As mentioned above, such a situation is to be expected, since it belongs to the very nature of historical freedom.

This uncertainty is no reason for giving up in the matter. It means that we can freely choose a course that may not a priori be considered impossible, that we can live with the resolve not to despair of the future of Europe but to safeguard it in its characteristic distinctiveness, even in the world's unknown future. Generally speaking, the full development of humanity does not consist in shaping a universal human being, who is everywhere the same, but rather in developing the open-minded and loving unity of all persons who, in the plurality of their distinctive characteristics, make up *the* human person. Hence the resolve to preserve Europe for the future, with its own values and peculiarities, should not be called a utopia or a meaningless selfishness that simply refuses to disappear into a uniform and homogenized world civilization. So the question that concerns us is no longer purely theoretical. It becomes an invitation to freedom, an invitation to undertake a struggle whose outcome is uncertain.

Moreover Christians at least can take heart from their theology of history, which tells them that something of Europe will continue to exist, even in its historical distinctiveness, insofar as Christianity will not perish in the world. Despite its universal appeal, and even because of it, Christianity can never deny, indeed it must always remember, its historical origin and even the way it has been historically transmitted. Now it happens that this transmission occurred through Europe. For the faith, which European Christians expect will become the faith to be found *in* the whole world (even if perhaps not the faith *of* the whole world), is the faith that must forever keep in touch with its origins, which took place in the West, in the very roots of the West. The Christianity of the future all over the world may (so we hope!) look quite different from European Christianity, because it will have taken root in totally different cultures and in the coming unified world civilization. Yet one of its characteristics will always remain its historical origin; it will always continue to speak of Europe, because the Christianity of the future, flourishing in other countries too, will not be an abstract idea, but a reality that has a history and that preserves its history.

VALUES AND NORMS OF EUROPE

This does not mean, of course, that only specifically Christian characteristics of European culture should be transmitted and be important in the future for the rest of the world. There are undoubtedly many other important human values and characteristics that have become history in Europe. They deserve to survive and to be important for the rest of the world. So again we have to tackle the question whether these European values have a prospect of survival and meaningfulness for the rest of the world *insofar as* they grow into universal values that may be understood and actualized equally well by all people, or whether they will in the future actually retain a European particularity and, in this way only, become significant for the rest of the world.

For there is no doubt that certain values and norms, which have become explicit and accepted in European history, have continued to develop. They became universal in such a way that they have also become values and norms in other cultures and societies outside of Europe. This is the case, for instance, with all the ideals and purposes that are intended by the words "universal human rights," "democracy," "women's liberation," and so on. In regard to these human values, this might lead us to think that the task of Europe means only that these values, which historically speaking are of European origin, continue to be valid for Europe and the rest of the world in their universal human significance. The process is like higher mathematics, which historically began in Europe but has now — at least at first sight — become equally well understood and valid everywhere. And thus it seems to have lost its erstwhile European provenance.

Yet one might say and therefore have the right to hope that in individual cultures, whose variety should continue to exist even in a common world civilization, these universal human values would in their turn keep their distinctive cultural stamp and become significant for other cultures precisely in their distinctiveness. In the narrower circle of interpersonal relations, we each act in *our* own way, which is *not* the way of others; we are all important for others, as incentives for their further development, as people whose opinion they value, and so on. All members of such a circle accept and welcome one another in their own distinctive way which embodies common shared humanity. Something similar can and should occur in the family of peoples and in world cultures. The different cultures and peoples might embody their common humanity in each one's distinctive manner, and in this way — not through a formal and abstract realization of their humanity in the most homogeneous way possible — serve other peoples and cultures.

Of course, the differences among the ways of embodying the universally human can also occasion the danger of mutual misunderstanding and conflict, as we see now all over the world, even where appeal is made to the highest human values and principles. Yet the purpose cannot be to render people as uniform as possible, in order to make such conflicts impossible. Time and again problems crop up with efforts that are constantly being made to reconcile what is common to all people with the various forms this common nature has assumed. Take, for instance, the frequent conflicts in Communist countries about the right relation between shared communist principles and the different ways in which these principles are applied in different countries. This is also true for Europe. Europe should keep its own way of embodying the humanity it shares with all others in all dimensions of a culture. And it is precisely in this way — and not by giving up its own distinctiveness — that it must make its own unique contribution to the common culture and future of humankind.

It is often difficult to realize the difference between the universally human as such and its concrete application in a given culture, and this for many reason. The bearers of something that is really universal may exaggerate the importance of the concrete way they embody and realize this universal value; they might consider it an essential part of the value and call it obligatory for all. On the other hand, it is possible to overlook or reject something that belongs to a universal value on the pretext that it originated in a certain historically contingent spot in history and can therefore have no universal validity. Finally it may happen that incomplete ways of embodying what is truly universal are nevertheless taken over by others, as they exchange values and styles, some of which have no universal value.

PART TWO

Ecumenism

6

REALISTIC POSSIBILITY OF
A UNIFICATION IN FAITH?

I would like to submit a few reflections about the as yet unrealized possibilities contained in our efforts for ecumenical unity. I wish to emphasize that these reflections are submitted in my own name, at my own risk, and that they might be rejected by the Protestant as well by the Catholic side.

All sides claim that ecumenical efforts can and must continue. Yet they seem to stagnate. Is it not allowable then to make suggestions, even if they seem bold or desperate? We are not looking merely for a greater rapprochement between the churches, although this is undoubtedly a worthwhile goal. Our goal is a real unity of the great Christian churches, a goal that seems to be out of reach. Efforts to bring it about seem to stagnate hopelessly. Yet we must seriously consider that efforts aiming at the goal itself, and not merely efforts for a greater rapprochement, are possible, since all Christians have received from their common Lord a command to realize this unity, a command to which they must attach the greatest importance. That is why new, almost utopian suggestions of how we might make progress should not be rejected out of hand as heretical or unrealistic.

The following considerations refer to the *dogmatic* aspect of the ecumenical problem. We do not consider here the practical problems and those that derive from canon law. This does not mean, of course, that they are not as important as the theological problems. Much more thought should be given to problems coming from canon law. It is indisputable that the one Church of the fu-

ture cannot come about through a simple assimilation of the great
Protestant or Orthodox churches into the Roman Catholic Church
as it is juridically organized in the Latin West. And it is obvious
that great obstacles will also have to be overcome in the practical life of the churches, both in their ordinary ways of looking at
things and in their unconscious moods and habits, if Christians of
all separated churches are to feel at ease, like brothers and sisters,
in the one Church. It stands to reason that the Church of the future
must make room for a broad pluralism in the practical aspects of
Christian life. However, as mentioned above, in these reflections
we are considering only the dogmatic side of the ecumenical problem, that is, the problem of how the one Church of the future can
hold and profess the same Christian faith.

THE FUNDAMENTAL THESIS OF THE DOGMATIC SIDE
OF THE ECUMENICAL PROBLEM

This thesis points out that the mentality of people today in spiritual
matters is quite different from that of former times. Of course, the
real substance of the Christian faith and that which the existing
churches have considered as belonging to it cannot have changed
and should not be given up. But the manner in which the faith of
the existing churches can be brought together into the one faith
of the Church of the future may be quite different from the way
we thought of this unity in faith during the controversies between
the churches.

   This fundamental thesis can be explained only if we go back
somewhat further to shed light on the spiritual climate in which
people of today, and therefore the churches as well, have to live.
We wish to describe this spiritual climate, to explain how it has
changed in the course of history, to contrast our present situation
with the situation in which all the controversies about church unity
used to take place, and which naturally lingers on to some extent in our time. It follows, of course, that a description of these
situations and of the differences among them will necessarily be
oversimplified, that the differences will be emphasized more than
those elements which are common and permanent, so that it will
be easy to raise objections against such a description.

   Yet I believe that what will be said about this topic is more or less correct and of decisive importance for the question of how, at the present time, a unity in faith may be envisaged and demanded.

THE PRESENT SPIRITUAL CLIMATE

How shall we describe today's spiritual climate in which the Christian faith must be proclaimed? How does it differ from the situation in the West when the churches broke away from one another?

Let me put this in a simple and straightforward way. Formerly, the spiritual material, so to speak, with which people worked was relatively limited, affording a general view of the whole. Although they disagreed about many things, especially in their philosophy of life, they rightly took it for granted that they could be mutually understood in their conversations and in their controversies. It was easy to get an overall view of the ideas with which one worked and argued. At least theologians on all sides could take it for granted that they were in command of their discipline and all the problems that it might entail. They could also take it for granted that they were able to make themselves understood by their opponents, who operated with the same very limited conceptual material and experiential data. All sides were convinced therefore that they knew what they were talking about. It does not matter whether this common self-understanding was "objectively" correct, or whether even then controversies arose from an unconscious difference in basic attitudes, fundamental presuppositions, and so on. The self-understanding was there. Catholics, for instance, said that there were seven sacraments, while Protestants denied it. Both of them took for granted that they understood themselves and their opponents, that they were not talking at cross purposes.

This common self-understanding, this homogeneity at the verbal and conceptual levels on which each side was operating, derived, of course, from a fairly widespread cultural unity and shared experience, both of them rather narrow and, as a whole, easy to keep in mind. It was like a conflict between brothers and sisters of the same family. Whatever could be known at that time could be known by an individual, at least by one of sufficient culture and learning. This was not the case with many others, the uneducated, the common people. But that hardly mattered. From the start they were condemned to keep quiet while learned people argued among themselves and to follow the opinion accepted by the authorities and the learned, wherever they lived.

The world view of an earlier cultural epoch was, insofar as it could be consciously verbalized, relatively simple and easy to grasp in its entirety. Or it became such again after short critical periods between spiritual epochs. Such a world view referred to a geographically and historically limited area. That is why it was easy to view it as a whole and not too difficult to defend it in controversies. In the spiritual domain the opponents played, so to speak, with a limited number of balls, and were able, even where the game consisted in a difference of opinions, to play it with skill. They were convinced that they knew exactly their own opinions and the opinions, which they rejected, of their opponents.

Today the situation as it existed at the time of the breakup of the churches (it has been described very roughly here) has changed considerably. We might even speak not only of a quantitative but also of a qualitative change, even if historically the change occurred slowly and has become noticeable only in the present.

Today we know infinitely more and, as a result (however paradoxical it may sound), each individual, even the most cultured and the most learned, becomes ever more ignorant. Books become ever more numerous, and nobody can read them all. The number of computers keeps growing, as does their input and output. It is still possible to try to build synthetic surveys that will make an otherwise uncontrollable amount of detailed knowledge available to an individual. But the data that can be stored in computers cannot be viewed and controlled in their entirety by the individual.

As an individual, one becomes ever more ignorant. One must rely more and more upon the knowledge of others, without being able to master and to control it. The more skilled and better educated people are, the more they notice how, in every dimension of life, they are in certain respects becoming more ignorant; they have to rely more and more on others. There are more and more experts for countless theoretical and practical questions who behave toward others as authorities used to act toward ignorant people. But these experts understand each other only with the greatest difficulty or not at all. And so they form a dissonant chorus of voices offering their knowledge and their wisdom to others. Everywhere in the world consensus in society tends to move away from an agreement about basic convictions to a consensus that consists merely in the identity of material needs and presuppositions. This situation derives ultimately from the fact that the mass of what can actually be known has become so unwieldy that it can no longer be synthesized in the simple way that used to be possible.

That is why, in comparison with former times, the boundaries between the educated and the uneducated become very unclear. Today there are no longer people who are really educated and others who are not. Today all are educated in some respect and very ignorant in others. The universal savant is extinct.

CONSEQUENCES FOR THE ECUMENICAL QUESTION

This situation affects theology as well. Here too, compared with former times, there is an enormous amount of knowledge available. Consequently the individual theologian, and a fortiori the individual Christian, becomes ever more ignorant in comparison to the total knowledge presently available in theology. Today the biblical scholar can no longer also be a systematic theologian to the extent required by systematic theology itself. The expert in the history of dogma, not without reason, mocks systematic theologians who play with many fewer balls than the history of dogma might offer them. Biblical studies has turned into such an exacting science, one that works with the most diverse methods, that even individual scholars realize that they are able to master only a small part of their own discipline. Of course, there still exist in theology people who try to perform the function of universal experts. Some even must try to do so if, for instance, they happen to belong to the small group in the Congregation of the Faith who have to watch over and judge the orthodoxy of other theologians.

It becomes more and more questionable whether and to what extent such a universal theological erudition can still be attained by an individual, especially since, in the humanities, technical scientific means are of little use. Theologians too know more and more, and that is why they can understand each other less and less. Individual theologians are becoming steadily less certain that they have understood other theologians. It can be assumed that other theologians can be correctly understood only if their presuppositions are kept in mind. And these presuppositions are no longer within reach. There are, of course, many theologians and church leaders who do not admit that such is the present situation in theology, who repress it, who are still trying to think and work as if the situation had not changed. In a certain sense, they even have the right to do so, since our right to understand others and even to judge whether they are right or wrong cannot be denied. Yet it must be honestly admitted that the present situation exists and that it differs qualitatively from the earlier one.

Before we examine what follows from this situation for the ecumenical question itself, we will say a few words about an epistemological problem. When one refrains from affirming a proposition that is certainly or possibly true one does not err. This obvious truth applies not only to cases where the persons in question do not know the proposition or do not understand it. They may know about it, understand it to some extent, and at the same time have serious reasons for refusing to admit it. These reasons do not necessarily have to derive from the actual inner difficulty of the proposition; they may be of another kind. The proposition may, for instance, be unimportant for the person's own situation; taking the trouble to verify its truth, before accepting it, would not be worth the effort. Or the proposition, while correct, may be presented in an unfamiliar terminology or context that makes it hard to understand. In such cases, one cannot say that a given proposition obliges one to give a positive and explicit assent, for the simple reason that one must take its truth into account. In certain cases one may respectfully leave the proposition alone, without infringing upon one's duty to honor the truth.

What is true for individuals applies, of course, to the larger group as well. In their case too a lack of existential interest in certain propositions may be lawful for other reasons, even when the propositions in question are not positively denied and when their truth should be taken into account.

What has been said in general is also true for the statements of a creed and for the people of a Church. It seems evident to me that, in practice, the churches (the Catholic Church too) accept what we have said, at least implicitly. When Christians have been baptized, when they lead a life that is to some extent Christian, the Church considers them legitimate members of the Christian community. The Church does not carefully inquire exactly what statements of the faith are explicitly present in their consciousness or to what extent they are aware of the complete dogma of the Church. She does not try to find out how they feel about certain things that she teaches and may even, in some historical situations, expressly proclaim. She is satisfied if, on the one hand, it is clear from the religious practice of these people that they evidently accept — even if only in a global and rudimentary way — the basic dogmas, the ultimate foundations in the hierarchy of truths of the faith, and if, on the other hand, they do not mentally or verbally explicitly reject statements that the Church claims objectively belong to the heart of the faith. The Church knows that in the individual consciousness of most of her members there exist plenty of religious and profane ideas that do not objectively agree with one another. She knows that, even where one of her members agrees with one of her statement, repeats and professes it, she herself cannot be absolutely certain that this person, when repeating this statement, really understands and accepts what the Church herself means by it.

All the churches, including the Catholic Church, are satisfied when their members live as baptized and practicing believers in a human, juridical, and liturgical unity and when they live up to the essential elements of the Christian faith. (This must be presumed for the external forum at least.) She does not require from every member an explicit assent to every statement which she herself considers part of her binding profession of faith. This epistemological, somewhat minimalistic, tolerance is quite unavoidable, and it is also legitimate in the churches.

THE UNITY OF THE CHURCHES

These considerations about the spiritual situation today, as contrasted with that of earlier times, allow us to say the following.

From the dogmatic point of view and with respect to the faith of the Church, unity of the separated churches is conceivable, if no Church declares that a statement held to be binding by another Church is absolutely irreconcilable with her own understanding of the faith. As long as such disagreements existed, or continue to exist, a unity of the churches in faith is naturally unthinkable. But do such discrepancies still exist? I am inclined to doubt it. Theological discussions among theologians of the different churches have not yet sufficiently come to the awareness of church leaders. It is certainly not that the theologians of the different churches who may seriously be considered as representing the faith consciousness of their respective churches (which does not apply to all those who pursue theology as the science of religion) have already reached a positive agreement among themselves in all dogmatic questions. But are there still many serious theologians around today who would declare that the statements which theologians in another confession consider absolutely binding on their Church are irreconcilable with the former theologians' own faith, the faith which they confess as decisive for salvation?

It is certain that in many questions or controversies theologians are not yet in total agreement. But the climate of their conversations has fundamentally changed in comparison with the time of the Reformation. Then they faced each other with positions which the other side always called objectively and absolutely irreconcilable with the foundations of Christianity. Salvation for the other side — if possible at all — was seen as possible only because, for some strange subjective reasons, the others were not responsible for their false doctrine, a doctrine whose falsity they might, with some good will, be able to recognize. Today theologians whose tenets may not yet be totally reconcilable take a different stance toward each other. Both sides take into account not only that a mysterious subjectivity exonerates at times the other before God and before the truth of the Gospel but also that the statements of both sides, when further developed and understood in a wider context, sometimes do not really contradict each other, even when one does not yet clearly see that, in such a wider interpretation, the two sides positively agree.

It seems to me that, in such a new situation, a sufficient unity in faith may have already been achieved among the churches. Protestants would not right away have to give a positive assent of faith to many propositions that Catholics consider binding in faith. Neither would they have to reject them because — as shown by historical development and by today's spiritual climate — they cannot say that accepting these specifically Catholic tenets would mean giving up their own faith, that it would mean denying truths that *they* rightly consider essential to their faith. Neither does the fact that they refrain from making a judgment about these tenets imply that they are moving toward the Catholic position. These Protestant Christians may assume that, in the ongoing history of the Church's faith-awareness, there is hope that these Catholic tenets will find a clarification and an interpretation that will allow a positive assent. Although they cannot assent at present, they should not feel obliged to reject Roman Catholic teachings out of hand.

On the other hand, it seems to me that the leadership of the Catholic Church could find this position acceptable for a unification of the churches. It implies that the properly fundamental truths of Christian revelation are expressly affirmed by both sides. But a positive assent is not required for every proposition that, in the historical development of the faith-awareness of the Roman Catholic Church, is considered to be objectively given with divine revelation. On their side, the Orthodox and Protestant churches may be willing to refrain from judging (as part of the faith) that some specifically Roman Catholic tenets are utterly irreconcilable with divine revelation and gospel truth, as they judged them at the time of the Reformation.

Suppose that both sides accept this kind of existential and epistemological tolerance, whereby that which is explicitly and expressly taught is not coerced into radical contradiction. There would still be leeway for those issues that, although not yet positively compatible, are admittedly reconcilable. In such a case it seems to me that, from the dogmatic point of view, church unity is possible right away.[1]

This statement may sound bold, utopian, perhaps even dogmatically vulnerable. But if one is unwilling to consider unification of the churches absolutely impossible in the present spiritual climate — something forbidden by the basic convictions of Christianity and the Church — then one would have to say that any unification in faith other than the one we have mentioned above is utterly impossible. The suggested approach could therefore be considered legitimate.

OTHER WAYS OF CONCEIVING UNITY

Let us imagine a more ideal and more radical unity of the churches, as always an obvious goal still dreamed of in ecumenical discussions. Let us imagine what this unification would look like if it were really brought about. Would theologians in today's spiritual climate

[1]See the recent important contribution to this topic by H. Fries and K. Rahner, *Unity of the Churches: An Actual Possibility* (Mahway, N.J.: Paulist Press, 1985). This book contains eight crucial theses about the ecumenical situation.

not continue to disagree? Would the faith formulas explicitly accepted by all not continue to be interpreted in very different ways? Would this not follow from the different intellectual horizons, with the different terminologies that would unavoidably continue to exist in this world characterized by cultural pluralism? Consider the narrow personal situation of many of the faithful. Would they not admit that they are not interested in some of the doctrines? Or would they not simply and quietly refrain from giving a positive assent to such doctrines? In an ideal unity of faith these things are not supposed to happen. In the unification we have suggested it would be admitted and legitimate.

What I mean is this: Either one makes of the unification of faith an ideal that is really unreachable and merely pays lip service to it, or one strives for a unification that is realistically possible and that should therefore be admitted as legitimate and rendered theologically understandable. In other words, the unity in faith that, for all practical purposes, exists and must be regarded as legitimate in the Catholic Church differs from the one that ecclesiology implicitly takes for granted and presupposes, and which implies (explicit or at least implicit) positive assent to all that church leadership teaches as a doctrine binding for faith.

Now the unity in faith that actually exists, even within the Catholic Church, differs from this theoretically postulated unity. Yet it is legitimate and should be explicitly acknowledged as such. It follows that for the unity in faith of the future world-Church, one should not demand more than the unity that exists in the Catholic Church, and that one should expressly acknowledge such unity as sufficient and legitimate. Of course, this conception of unity should also be admitted as sufficient by the Orthodox and Protestant churches. But that should cause no difficulty, since it is easy to see that, even at the present, they are already satisfied with the unity that we consider sufficient for the one Church of the future. In this respect, the only requirement is that these other churches should not positively reject an explicit doctrine of the Catholic Church as irreconcilable with the foundations of their Christianity.

To my mind such a development of ecclesial consciousness has made so much progress that this situation has become possible, although probably not for every individual Christian or theologian in these churches. But one can admit that a majority of individual Christians and theologians in the other churches will no longer anathematize specific Roman Catholic doctrines in the name of faith, so that the leadership in these churches will not anathematize them either. This being granted, it seems to me that there is no need to demand that these churches give a positive assent of faith to specific Roman Catholic teachings and that a sufficient unity of faith may be reached among those who, confessing the triune God and Jesus as Lord and Savior, believe the essential foundations of Christianity and have been baptized. The main thesis that I dared to present points out therefore that in today's spiritual climate no greater unity of faith can be reached than the one I suggested, that this unity must therefore be legitimate if, despite all assurances to the contrary, one does not want to give up the hope of such a unity of the churches in faith.

FURTHER UNSOLVED QUESTIONS

Even if one accepts this theory, much arduous reflection is still needed for a real unity of the churches; many problems remain to be solved. Not much thought has yet been given on all sides to the question of how the Church of the future will look *juridically*, so that church unity may be a real possibility. It stands to reason that there can be no question of the Protestant and Orthodox churches simply disappearing into the Roman Catholic Church, while the latter would simply remain as she is, with her own liturgy, canon law, manner of appointing bishops, and Roman Curia with all its various functions.

Of course, more reflection is required to find out how exactly this, as it were, more prudent and discreet unity can be maintained and lived in the Church of the future. For in the future too some juridical organization will undoubtedly be required for that purpose. Even today there exists in Germany's Protestant churches the possibility of proceedings for enforcing doctrinal orthodoxy. This shows that the Church of the future should be enabled to defend herself against serious errors that threaten the essentials of her faith, exclude fundamental heresies that will, of course, also be possible in the future. But the concrete juridical way in which the faith of the Church is presented and defended does not have to be the one used today in the Roman Catholic Church.

Along with this necessary and sufficient unity in faith, the Church of the future will be characterized by a greater pluralism in the laws of individual churches, as well as in Christian life, liturgy, and theology than had been allowed in the Roman Catholic Church. In this respect the Roman Catholic Church could learn from her relationship to the small Uniate churches of the East and take over a few things that could serve as a model for this lawful pluralism in the Church of the future. But this pluralism in the Church of the future will undoubtedly have to be broader than the one we Roman Catholics are used to, especially since the pluralism that has been accepted as basically legitimate among us, on account of the Uniate Eastern churches, has hardly had any practical effects on Western Christians and the Roman Curia.

Orthodox and Protestant partner churches, without positively rejecting as contrary to the faith the dogmatic teaching of the First Vatican Council, have not expressly taken it over into their understanding of faith. A difficult question therefore for theory and practice will be how this fact can be reconciled with a concrete acknowledgment, translated into practice, of the function of the Petrine office. This is so especially since no one can forbid the Roman See to exercise that fullness of teaching power that Vatican I attributes to it.

But if the Roman papacy were expressly to promise that, should it ever wish to proclaim a definition *ex cathedra*, it would use a procedure through which practically, even without a real council, such a definition would be based on the assent of the bishops of all partner churches, this most delicate problem might also be solved. In that way the Orthodox or Protestant churches in the Church of the future would not get the impression that any kind of acceptance of the Petrine function would at once deliver them so much to the doctrinal authority of Rome that there would be a real danger that their own awareness of the faith might be jeopardized.

IMPORTANCE OF THE ECUMENICAL MOVEMENT

Even if one were ready to accept the suggested main thesis, the road leading to the unity of all Christian churches would naturally be long, not only for the reasons mentioned above. The churches, should, in their practice and mentality, get used to one another even more than they have up to the present, so that a visible unity may become possible and achievable. That is why all great and small ecumenical endeavors are very important. Even if they are made with some skepticism about the possibility of a real unity of the churches, they bring us ever closer to this unity.

Christians of the different denominations come closer to each other through such endeavors; they really get to know each other; they become aware of the fact that they are already united in the essential elements of the Christian faith. The feeling of unfamiliarity and indifference that has prevailed among them is decreasing. And so the day may slowly dawn when the churches will in fact wonder: Do we not, after all, have the same Christian faith? Can we not confess it together in greater unity without straining the conscience of the churches that have until now been separated?

By way of conclusion I would say: If we take into account the diversity of the partner churches and the tolerance in matters of faith that will be required and even legitimate in the Church of the future, and if we then compare this Church of the future with the present situation among the churches, we will have to admit that our present ecumenical situation is not as bad as one might at first be tempted to think. The partner churches of the one Church of the future may show very important differences in their way of life. But so does our own Church nowadays. Therefore the present situation in our Church does not differ as much as we might think from the one Church of the future, which will include a great diversity among its partners. As ecumenical convergence continues, we may suddenly notice that we are already much closer to each other than we had thought and than we give credit for to the churches.

7

CONCRETE OFFICIAL STEPS TOWARD UNIFICATION

Not all properly theological questions that are considered controversial by the Christian churches have been answered with full agreement on all sides. Yet it does seem that today the unification of the churches must become mainly a concern of church leaders. They can no longer plead the fact that, since theologians do not yet agree, they themselves have, for the time being, nothing to do but utter a few friendly words of ecumenical good will. Is it not possible for these church leaders to do something tangible right now? Let me try to say something about this question with respect to the Roman Catholic Church. Two things come to mind.

First, concrete problems of an interconfessional nature that occur today in pastoral work might be reexamined and courageously solved. Germany's Protestant churches have already requested this of the Catholic Church in Germany, but they have had no concrete and encouraging answer. Would it not be possible, with regard to intercommunion, to make new arrangements that the Catholic side has not yet dared to make? Would it not be possible for a Catholic who has married a Protestant to fulfill his or her "Sunday obligation" by attending a Protestant Sunday service occasionally? Would it not be possible to agree upon a more broadminded cooperation among the churches for the education of children of "mixed marriages?" Would it not be possible to invent cooperative ventures in religious education that could be shared by both churches? After all, this education as it now exists can impart little more than the understanding and practice of the most fundamental Christian convictions, and these are shared by both churches.

An answer to these practical questions of pastoral care that is as ecumenical as possible is imperative for both churches and must be found. Certainly Catholic theologians may have to confront limits that cannot be crossed, although the other side would like to see them crossed and believes that it can be done. Have these limits, in theory or in practice, already been reached on the Catholic side? Ecumenically speaking, is it now impossible to go further? I see no proof that it is not.

Furthermore there are many questions about the Church's self-understanding, about canon law and canonical procedures that are ecumenically of great importance and that might be answered by the Catholic Church in a different and better way. The answers to such questions should not be postponed until the time of unification, but should be given as they come up, clearly, officially, and as partial steps toward complete church unity. We should avail ourselves of these possibilities not only in very general declarations of principles, or in non-binding statements of theologians, but in official declarations. In this way, we would make credible our real resolve to make ecumenical progress.

Why should the Holy See not declare right away, every time a case comes up, the possibilities it sees for a real unity of the churches, the possibilities it is willing to grant? This would not imply that, in theory and practice, the Protestant churches would simply and uniformly be taken over by the Latin Church of the West. Or what juridical ways of finding and appointing a bishop are possible that, while differing considerably from the procedure prescribed by the present Roman canon law, still agree with Catholic dogma and might more easily be accepted by the Protestant churches? During the Council the bishops of the Uniate churches of the Near East declared that they were willing to resign at once if the Orthodox churches entered into union with Rome. Would it not be possible for Rome officially to make arrangements like this obligatory in principle?

Such partial but binding agreements would be possible in the domain of dogmatic theology itself. For instance, would it not be possible for the magisterium to make a declaration about the Mass as a sacrifice that would do away with the misgivings of Protestants who believe that Catholics consider the Mass a repetition, not merely a rendering present, of the sacrifice of the cross? Would it not be possible to make a magisterial declaration, clearer even than that of the Council of Trent, to the effect that every justifying human activity is supported by the free, gratuitous action of God's grace and that every good free human action is itself a grace of God, that we reject a naive synergism? Would it not be possible to make officially clear that an *ex cathedra* decision of the pope is, outside a council, of its very nature an exception and occasioned by particular circumstances? Could it also be made clear that such a decision today, when worldwide communications facilitate the Church's search for truth, will take place in such a way that it is practically a conciliar decision, because the whole Church has cooperated in its elaboration? Hence, if Protestant Christians should recognize the First Vatican Council, they would not have to fear papal decisions that might take them by surprise and demand too much from them. Would it not be quite simple to expound, even officially, a doctrine of the sacraments that would not make people think of magic and sorcery? Would it not be possible to describe the required conditions for a sacramental intention in marriage in such a way that one might more clearly and easily notice the absence of such an intention, so frequent nowadays in civil marriages? These are only a few examples. There are certainly many others that will not be mentioned here.

The conclusions of every theological dialogue among the Christians churches during the last few decades should be published officially. Otherwise, the theological interchurch dialogue does not have the effect that it might have; rather, there is much talk with no tangible results. The importance of developing an awareness that consists in more mutual trust and that aims at practical intercommunion should not be underestimated. But this general awareness will lead to a real unification of the churches only if it can take shape in detailed dogmatic statements. They should be made not only in the ongoing theological discussions that are influenced by theological trends but they should also become statements of the magisterium.

The magisterium of the Catholic Church may not only define doctrines, it may also make authentic statements. Today it must have the courage to use its possibilities, not just through admonitions and restrictions that betray a lack of ecumenism, but through ecumenical measures aiming at unification. When in its encyclicals, for instance, the magisterium not only rejects errors but also positively proclaims the Christian truth, one cannot a priori hold that the Congregation of the Faith has only a supervisory function that expresses itself by rejecting heterodox or dangerous doctrines. The Congregation of the Faith might also, in collaboration with the Secretariat for Unity, propose positive doctrines that contain the results of interchurch discussions among theologians. Only then will one get a concrete idea of what has already been achieved, and of what is still to be achieved in the quest for dogmatic unity.[1]

It seems to me that the Protestant churches too must do some of the things that are here suggested to the Catholic Church. Could they not declare that one has not betrayed the pure grace of God in Jesus Christ if one accepts the Council of Trent's doctrine of justification? But here again the old difficulty comes up. Who can speak with binding power for Protestant Christians?

It seems to me that our ecumenical efforts should little by little produce concrete results. Interchurch commissions, proceedings of private groups without official binding power, all fall short of the results that are more and more expected today.

---

[1]See on this H. Fries, "Das Petrusamt in anglikanish-katholischen Dialog," in *Stimmen der Zeit* 200 (1982) 723–38. This article has been written in agreement with K. Rahner.

8

ECUMENICAL TOGETHERNESS
TODAY

I n what follows I would like to submit a couple of simple considerations about the question of ecumenical unity: Here and now
at a time when the ultimate goal of all ecumenical endeavors
has not yet been reached, what must Christians and their churches
do to get closer to that goal and to overcome a certain stagnation, resignation, and listlessness, which seem to be hampering the
progress of ecumenical work?

As we try to address that question, it is obvious that only a couple
of fragments of an answer can be presented, and that we must
formulate them not so much as demands made to church leaders
on both sides, but as demands made to ourselves, the Christian
rank and file.

RADICALIZATION IN THE DIRECTION OF JESUS CHRIST

The first and in fact the most important demand involves the invitation to all Christians, in all churches, to become more intensively,
more radically Christian. In its innermost core Christianity is not
a theory, joined to a harmonious way of life, which has been transmitted once and for all and which we have accepted and now
continue to confess and practice. Real Christianity is spirit and life,
a readiness to be overtaxed, a constant new beginning, a pilgrimage
that has not yet reached its definitive home, a willingness always to
welcome new experiences. Clearly, then, it would be preposterous

and un-Christian for the Christian churches simply to carry on, conservatively, in their traditional *status quo*. They can keep their lawful inheritance for the future only if they are willing to change. They must be attuned to their times. This does not mean that everything is allowed, that alien fashions are arbitrarily accepted. It means an ever renewed and radical return to the innermost heart of the faith, to which both Christians and the churches must bear witness. Christians must become more Christian; then automatically they will come closer to each other. What is required is not a liberalizing diluting of Christianity into a worldwide humanism.

From the time of the Enlightenment, theology and science in the Western world have discovered many truths that are now taken for granted. They should be quietly accepted by the churches. It has been shown, time and again, and ever more clearly, that none of this threatens or questions a radical Christian faith, that the natural sciences, the historical sciences, the historical-critical approach to the Bible, and even a modern sense of the world and of life can really be combined with a genuine Christian faith. That is why in all churches a lively Christianity, which lives ever more intensively from the roots of its faith, is a task that is possible today and required for the sake of ecumenism. True, we cannot simply eliminate by arbitrary decree the old problems of theological controversy among the Christian churches, nor can we call the controversies irrelevant. But all of them would acquire new perspectives and a fresh impact. It would be possible to confront and master them and to solve them together, if they were pondered within the common task of the churches and of Christians, a task that consists of understanding and practicing original, genuine, truly orthodox Christianity, as it grapples with the common problems of our time.

Do we Christians not all confess the ultimate, real incomprehensibility into which we are plunged and which we call God? And with a boldness that finds no justification in ourselves, do we not dare to speak to this uncontrollable incomprehensibility, have dealings with it and trust it, convinced that we are sheltered in it, accepted by it, that we arrive at it in the bottomless pit of our death, and that we are absolved by it as it promises itself to us? Are we not the ones who venture upon this dreadful journey called faith as we look at Jesus and the abyss of his death on the cross, recognizing him as the one who is saved, and accepting because of him the invincible conviction that we too, without being destroyed, will blessedly attain the one whom Jesus calls his Father and to whom he yielded himself unconditionally, while feeling utterly forsaken by him? Have we not all let Jesus tell us the first, the last, and the supreme word, in which God promises himself to us as our goal and our end, as our judgment and our reconciliation? Have we not all been baptized in this final word of God in Jesus, so that — whether we want it or not — we already enjoy, through baptism, a basic unity in the Spirit and in the tangibleness of social testimony? If we remember these realities and if we live them more radically, then slowly and inexorably a unity in faith and belief will grow. Over and above the unity that already exists, this unity will give rise to a community of faith, the goal of the ecumenical movement.

It seems possible for a Christianity that is lived from its innermost core to achieve unity in the doctrines that are to some extent secondary and in which the churches still feel that they are not yet united. Or it may become clear that the apparently controversial statements of the different churches do not really cancel each other out, but rather are attempts to elucidate the inexhaustible fullness of Christianity from different points of view. The attempts to harmonize the theologies of the Christian churches have been very successful during the past few decades. In almost all the major churches — not always in the others — there are theologians who hold that in theological controversy there are no longer any differences of opinion that should really *separate* the churches. These theologians think that church leaders should now draw the appropriate consequences from this state of affairs, and that they should not, through canon law or otherwise, maintain divisions that no longer exist theologically. The opinion of such theologians may be somewhat too optimistic and ahead of the facts. But it does show that a return to the basic substance of Christianity in the context of a courageous encounter with today's world and a reexamination of the old problems of theological controversy from that point of view may be very important and promising for ecumenism.

The presupposition is, of course, that church leaders feel responsible not only for the past of their churches but even more for their future. The presupposition is that contemporary Christianity is not just theoretically known but practically lived. Here lies our greatest deficiency. If Christians not only thought their truth but lived it, if they were as concerned for orthopraxy as for orthodoxy, if this orthopraxy meant not only social criticism and social change (although here too we notice how frightfully wanting narrowminded conservatism is) but worshipping God in spirit and in truth, since we exist for God and not God for us, then they would soon be able to agree about controversial theological questions that, like it or not, no longer have the same importance as at the time of the Reformation. They are now of secondary importance, not because they would be such in their deepest meaning — grace and justification are not in themselves of secondary importance — but because today we must view such topics in a much wider context, and against a much deeper background. The answers therefore, necessarily display more nuances and can converge more easily than was formerly the case.

NO THIRD CONFESSION

A second maxim that is important today in ecumenical work might be formulated as follows: It is meaningless and even, in the long run, harmful for ecumenical work, when practical ecumenical projects are conducted with so much speed that something like a third confession is created. Ecumenical services are good and Christians may work together harmoniously in the most diverse undertakings. I myself have no objection if a married couple from two churches, when their conscience and their love urges them, attend the same divine service, and eventually the same celebration of the Lord's Supper. But agreements that simply ignore or deny the still existing differences in faith and canon law do not lead toward Christian unity. In both churches the majority of Christians will not take part in such moves, with the result that these efforts lead to a new split, some kind of third confession. Then we have Protestant Christians, Catholic Christians, and overeager ecumenists, who wrongly believe that the Christianity that they practice is the fullness of Christianity and a sufficient foundation of unity. At present such a self-evaluation by these ecumenists may be quite understandable. Yet it amounts to overestimating oneself and ignoring the Christian past and the faith of former times, which we may not give up for the sake of some cheap unity but must introduce into the genuine and complete unity of the Church of the future.

It is quite true that all churches must get rid of much historical baggage if they seriously desire the coming unity. With all due respect to church leaders, we have to wonder, not without fear and worry, whether they really possess enough ecumenical resolve and daring. Yet it is impossible to establish unity by being indifferent to the faith of former times, by building unity on the basis of a minimal content of faith, about which one is not quite sure whether it still is specifically Christian. We cannot simply set aside legitimate church authority and its directives in order to attain a unity of a new splinter group. Efforts toward unity should try to comprise *all* Christians, even those who more traditionally identify with the present condition of the transmitted creeds and churches. Unity must be realized *with*, not against, church authorities. The road to such unity may be longer and harder. But building an awareness in the churches that can later bring about and bear a genuine unity cannot be the product of a liberalism that is, after all, just a passing fashion. It must be the product of a real history of faith. That is very difficult and supposes great patience. All of this should not be used by authorities and by lazy Christians as a theological pretext for doing nothing and for putting off the unity of the churches to the day of eternity. But if the ecumenical movement should lead to the establishment of a third confession, it would have missed its goal and produced division instead of unity.

AGAINST CONFESSIONALISM

A third maxim for today's ecumenism might be formulated as follows: Are not some obstacles to unity in reality only creations of a narrow confessionalism? It is quite possible that, until recently, Roman prelates could imagine a union of the Roman Catholic Church and the Protestant Church in Germany only in the following way: Protestant-Christians would return to the Catholic Church through massive individual conversions, as it were, whereupon they would be subject to Rome just like lifelong Catholics. For Rome the way in which the churches of the West would be unified (the East is a different case) could be conceived, insofar as they tried to conceive it at all, only as a surrender of the other churches to the Roman Church. The latter would remain unchanged, only growing in numbers. I might ask whether fervent Reformed Christians from Geneva would imagine that the Catholic Church of the future, should it be united with their Church, would become like that Church: sober and without images, temples of the word, not of sacrament. Such imagined models of the coming unity, which have prevailed unconsciously on both sides and still exist today, are obstacles to unity. For a genuine Christian faith they are mere fantasy.

Unity does not mean uniformity. The chimera of uniformity is a big obstacle to ecumenical activity. I cannot help thinking that Rome has not yet clearly, and in concrete details, explained what she would be willing and able to give up, without damage to her faith, for the sake of unity. I would ask whether a similar willingness to yield would not in many respects be possible on the Protestant side.

In her canon law the Catholic Church already admits several jurisdictions in the same territory; it cannot therefore be impossible a priori for her to admit, in the same territory, the existence of several partner churches with a different past history, which remain distinct while nevertheless living in the unity demanded by faith and love. We have, for instance, in the Catholic Church in Germany, a special jurisdiction for the Ukrainians, with its own hierarchy and liturgy, which lives nevertheless in unity and peace with Rome. Why would it not be possible to have, in Hesse, a diocese of "old" Catholics, with Mainz as episcopal see, and alongside it a united Hessian Church, whose historical origin and valid traditions date from the time of the Reformation? A certain amount of creative imagination and spiritual freedom is required in order to envisage something of the kind for the future. But might not such virtues be expected of us, Christians of today and of tomorrow? It stands to reason that both the decision to live in unity and church unity itself must be translated into practice and ensured by a number of juridical norms and laws. This can be done. However, the creation of a unity that includes different churches should by no means imply that the one Church, without changing herself, would lord it over the others and simply absorb them.

To my mind one might even, in this connection, give some thought to the question of whether the unity of faith that is naturally required allows not only for a considerable pluralism in the theologies of the individual partner churches but also for a diversity in the hierarchy of religious truths that are held in these churches. For instance, would a united Hessian Church have to celebrate the feast of the Assumption, or might this be foregone? In Rome's relation to the Uniate churches of the Near East, many major and minor paradigms can be found for the different ways in which a partner Church may be united with Rome, ways that differ considerably one from the other. Rome has apparently seen no insuperable obstacles to unity because of the regional and geographical differences between West and East in the Catholic Church. Although in the Christian churches of the West the geographical separation does not occur, it is not clear why the different historical development of these churches of the West might not give them the same right to a lasting differentiation.

GETTING TO KNOW THE OTHER CONFESSIONS

A fourth maxim might go like this: Get to know each other really well! This maxim sounds utterly obvious. All Christians tell the registry office to what denomination they belong; on the street they see the churches of other denominations; they know that these other denominations are communities of Christians with the same baptism they have received themselves and have the same kind of church organization they know in their own Church. A mixed marriage among their acquaintances gives rise to personal and canonical problems that bring home to them more clearly the pluralism of Christian creeds and confessions.

One would like to believe that this fourth maxim is a necessary presupposition of all ecumenical activities, one that, as a rule, is always and everywhere fulfilled. In fact this is not true. Even today it is still the case that, with regard to other churches, one knows only what can be seen of them in public, what is therefore not especially important for Christian existence itself. Christians who are fully committed to their own Church know little or nothing about the other churches, except some rather insignificant details. They live in the sacred purview of their own Church, they are (we hope) in touch with the pastors of their Church. If they are not theologians, their religious reading matter is more or less supplied only by their own churches (we readily grant that of late there are exceptions to this rule). On close examination, Christians committed to the life of their own Church know little of the properly religious and Christian life of the other churches. There is no reason to consider this as simply wrong, since a historically conditioned position belongs to each person's life. But today we must broaden our knowledge and experience of the life of our fellow Christians in the other churches.

What matters in this respect is not so much an increase of theoretical knowledge about the other churches as a vivid experience of the concrete Christian life of these other Christians. Otherwise the real chasm between the churches today, the main obstacle to unity of Christians, will not be bridged. For it consists not so much in differences among controverted theological opinions stemming from the past as in the feeling of unfamiliarity with a different religious style of life and in the inability to share that other life spontaneously and naturally. From the point of view of theology and faith, that unfamiliarity may be wholly unimportant, yet practically it is a greater obstacle than all the theological disagreements at the time of the Reformation. Many Protestant Christians will consider the Catholic sign of the cross or a May devotion unacceptable. A Catholic may find the prayer offered by a Protestant pastor pathetic and unctuous. These and a thousand similar differences in the daily life of the churches do not have any theological significance, yet they impede the work of the ecumenical movement. All of us still have much to learn in this respect. We have to acquire a concrete understanding of the way in which Christians of other churches live their Christianity.

It is good but not enough that during the last few decades the number of hymns shared by all Christian churches in Germany has increased, that in public meetings of Catholics and Protestants a speaker from another Church is invited, that in problems in which the churches confront the State or public opinion they adopt a common stand, and so on. The feeling of unfamiliarity and mutual indifference must still be overcome at the grass roots level among individual Christians in their daily lives. It is not easy to say how this should be done, since we can hardly use official directives for this purpose. Those who preach should try to listen to themselves with one ear, as it were, to find out whether what they say would be accepted by Christians of another Church, or would be understood as un-Christian. The same is also true for those who organize a liturgical service for their own Church. Each time they too should ask themselves whether this service would also be acceptable to a

Christian of another Church. That is why joint ecumenical services should not merely be tolerated as exercises required by ecumenical good will. They should be humble and brave attempts really to adore God with Jesus in spirit and truth, and to do it together with others better than they can do it alone.

Have we been brave and impartial enough in our attempts to consider the possibility of sharing divine services in places where, for lack of a priest or for other reasons, a service is impossible in one's own Church? Can a Christian not meaningfully make of the church of another denomination a place for private prayer and quiet recollection? Would any harm be done if, in the meeting room of a rectory, both one's own diocesan paper and current religious literature of other churches were on display? Are we still not much too prudent and cautious about tasks shared by the churches in the secular and public domain? In mixed marriages or when the question of the child's baptism comes up, is more attention not being paid to a precise drawing of limits than to unity? Shared practical ecumenical activities, like those of "Action 365," for instance, are not sufficiently emphasized in the average life of the churches. Opposing parties cannot be united if they do not understand each other; they cannot understand each other if they do not know each other; they cannot get to know each other if, out of distrust or indifference, they do not cultivate contacts through which alone they can come to know each other, and finally discover that they are all Christians, able to live in the one large and comprehensive Church of Jesus Christ, in the Church that, from its very nature and not merely by way of concession, comprises a wealth of regional and historically conditioned partner churches, because this is the only way in which the richness of Christ can become manifest in the world.

THE PRESENT UNITY

A last maxim: In order to achieve the unity of Christians, as we are enjoined to do, we should also rejoice on account of the unity that God has already bestowed on us. Have we all not been baptized in the name of the triune God? Do we all not try to live by the merciful grace of God, which we have received without any merit or title of our own? Do we all not read in the word of both Testaments the word of God himself, which judges and pardons us? Do we all not celebrate, as well as we can, the commemoration of the death of Jesus, until the day when the transforming power of this death will become wholly manifest and put an end to history? With the crucified Jesus, do we all not try to take up our own death into the incomprehensibility of God and of our own life? Are we Christians not convinced that in the struggle for justice and freedom in the world we have a frightful task that we have not yet completed? Are these not indications of a unity among Christians that has already been granted to us?

It is not true therefore that we Christians differ as much from each other in our world view and lifestyle as we differ from other political, social, and cultural groups in the world. But it is true that the unity which already unites all of us is not yet being fully used for the good of the whole world. As Christians, we already possess a unity given to us by God, which should fill us with a deep gratitude and joy. But we must also keep a few important things in mind. Even ecumenical unity that, as our proper task, is still ahead of us cannot and should not suppress considerable pluralism in the one Church. Such a pluralism will continue to be both a burden and a temptation in a unified Church of Christ. Even in a unified Church we will have to bear mutual lack of understanding, antagonism, and the like. Even a united Church cannot anticipate within history the blessed unity of the final kingdom of God.

But if we keep this humbly and soberly in mind, if we know that even a possible and necessary unity of Christians cannot anticipate here on earth the realm of eternal peace, and if we hope, with an optimism that comes from God, that God's grace can bring good even out of human sin and failure, that God can write straight with crooked lines and produce out of disunity a fullness of Christianity that could not have been reached through unity, then we may calmly and gratefully rejoice because of the imperishable unity that God has already granted to Christians. This joy should not turn into an excuse for a resigned stagnation of ecumenical activities. But those who do their share of this work, even if it is small and humble, may, in the glory of God's mighty grace, rejoice because of the unity that has already been granted to us Christians by God.

PART THREE

The Future of the Church

9

FORGOTTEN
DOGMATIC INITIATIVES OF
THE SECOND VATICAN COUNCIL

In connection with this topic I intend to consider only dogmatic themes. The Council's intent was to be a pastoral council and that is what it was. Its strongest and most far reaching suggestions referred to the homiletic and pastoral fields and to the strategy of a Church that has now become a world-Church. I will not take them up here. I speak of "initiatives." That means that the Council did not clearly and explicitly teach and interpret doctrines of a dogmatic sort; rather, it said things that are a start, a suggestion, an invitation to further dogmatic reflection and elaboration. Therefore I cannot quote any clear and unquestionable doctrines of the Council for my purpose. I can only point to conciliar statements that lead theologians to new questions requiring further reflection. These questions are important for preaching the faith now and in the future, although they have not yet received a clear answer that is generally accepted in the theology of the Church.

The title of this chapter speaks of "forgotten" initiatives. That does not mean, of course, that I am the only one who thinks of them. That would clearly be nonsense. What I mean is that, to my mind, they have generally not yet received sufficient attention and elaboration in current Catholic theology. I will not mention all possible initiatives. Important and unimportant ones are mentioned at random. I will start with a question that is not unimportant and that will shed light on the formal method of our considerations.

ATHEISM AND PERSONAL GUILT

Fifty years ago, when I was studying theology, we young theologians were taught as certain doctrine that in the long run positive atheism could not exist in a person without grave personal guilt. There is no need to explain at length what influence such a doctrine would have on the way in which Catholics might treat an atheist in their environment if the doctrine were applied to daily life. For this doctrine, the existence of God was so clear and so easy to demonstrate from reason, and the concept *God* in the statement "God exists" so obvious that, given normal intelligence and sufficient length of time, only a scoundrel could fail to be convinced of the existence of God. According to this doctrine nowadays we could be sure that we live among countless scoundrels and draw appropriate conclusions for our daily conduct.

During the Council nobody ever mentioned this traditional doctrine, not even the most conservative bishops and theologians; nor was it mentioned in the context of the conciliar debates and deliberations, where one would have expected it to come up. No serious discussions arose when the Council said: "Nor does divine Providence deny the help necessary for salvation to those who, without blame on their part, have not yet arrived at an explicit knowledge of God, but who strive to lead a good life, thanks to His Grace" (*Lumen Gentium*, 16). Or elsewhere when the Council, speaking of "all persons of good will in whose hearts grace works in an unseen way," says: "We ought to believe that the Holy Spirit in a manner known only to God offers to every human being the possibility of being associated with this paschal mystery" (*Gaudium et Spes*, 22).

I believe that a hundred years ago few theologians would have dared to make these and other statements of the Council about atheism and atheists. For the average person in the street today such declarations may sound utterly obvious. For a Church that is resolved at all costs to be faithful to both divine revelation and tradition, such statements in the history of her awareness of the faith are milestones to which she will not return. While positive atheism is always objectively false and a dreadful danger for a person's salvation, it cannot, as concretely present in human consciousness, simply and absolutely be identified with a deadly guilt to which

God can react only by a no of damnation. The Church admits also (not only!) a guiltless atheism, at least insofar as individuals in their own salvation history are concerned. So she must also — I say also — admit a positive significance of atheism for salvation at the same time as she fights unbelief in today's world. But with the declarations mentioned above the Church has reached a point in her awareness of the faith that she had not reached before, and she has clarified a position from which a really loving dialogue may be held with all people in the world.

When we consider what has been said, two things become clear. First, formally speaking, in the teaching of the Council on such dramatic questions we must pay attention to the things that are only hinted at or suggested by what has been omitted, even though they are of great importance. And secondly, such suggestions are an initiative for further reflection in theology. The tolerance of the Council, which does not deny that atheists as individuals may be guiltless before God, does not mean that everything here is clear, peaceful, and able to be solved in a liberal way. Rather, theologians are confronted with a pressing and difficult question that requires their attention. They cannot, in a sort of cheap liberalism, take it for granted that persons who have reached the age of reason and can make moral decisions can simply go on living free from guilt before God and enter into God's immediacy in eternal life without having known God.

Are there such guiltless atheists? Given the historical development that has led to the spiritual climate of today and tomorrow, it is hard to doubt it. Then the question comes up how, despite their professed atheism, they can have a real knowledge of God that leads to salvation and renders faith possible, although that faith is hidden, in the foreground of their consciousness, behind the atheism that they express in words. We are facing the problem of an anonymous theism, although quite a number of theologians detest the word "anonymous" in this connection. The word does not matter; what matters is the reality indicated by the statement of the Council, which brings up other more general questions of anthropology in theology as well. There must be more dimensions to human consciousness in its knowing and free decision-making, more foreground and background, more data, verbalized or not, accepted or repressed, than traditional theology has explicitly recognized.

RELATION OF THE TEACHING AND JURISDICTIONAL PRIMACY OF THE POPE TO THE FULLNESS OF POWER OF THE COLLEGE OF BISHOPS

Here is another initiative that gives us food for thought: the question of the precise relation, in theory and practice, between the universal teaching and jurisdictional primacy of the pope and the same fullness of power that belongs to the college of bishops — with and under the pope to be sure, but really to the college of bishops as such. The Council made a declaration, which had never before been made in a council, about the college of bishops as the highest bearer of the fullness of all sacramental and canonical power in the Church. The declaration led to rather intense discussions during the Council, although in fact it did not go beyond what the theologians of the First Vatican Council had said. It is known that Pope Paul VI watched anxiously lest the declaration about the nature and the function of the college of bishops overshadow the doctrine of Vatican I about the pope's supreme and universal primacy of jurisdiction and the fullness of his teaching power. These two teachings of the Council are now juxtaposed; both are of equal importance and validity. But the question of how these two subjects endowed with the fullness of power in the Church are related to each other remained unanswered in the Second Vatican Council. For theology, it is something that demands further study. It is easy to see that this question is of great importance for the life of the Church. Yet it looks as though theologians, canon lawyers, and church leaders do not consider it very difficult and worrisome.

In a single society there cannot exist two different subjects endowed with the fullness of power, because this would do away with the unity of the society. We might say however that this is not the case here, because the college of bishops is the bearer of the fullness of power only with and under the pope, so that there can be no question of an adequate distinction between the two subjects of this power. While this statement is true, it removes neither in theory nor in practice the problem brought up for theology and canon law by these two declarations.

In order to reconcile the two declarations it seems to me that we should start by emphasizing that, even when the pope acts on his own in matters of doctrine or law, he exercises his fullness of power *as* head of the universal episcopate. Otherwise the latter, not being identical with the pope, would be degraded to the rank of an advisory board in the universal Church. The pope's fullness of power must always and everywhere — even when he "acts alone" (which he may do of course) — be integrated into that of the body of bishops. And this body too cannot be understood aside from the unique power of the pope. Even if we hold this speculatively, it does not solve the problem for either theory or practice. The theoretical and practical problems met by Rome in the postconciliar synods of bishops are well known.

Pope Paul VI decided to organize these synods and intended to go on holding them, in order to live up to the teaching and the spirit of the Council about the college of bishops. We should not be surprised that the pope did not want to grant to a synod the rights and full powers of a council, either in theory or in practice. So, up to now, synods have been only meetings of an advisory body, while the pope has reserved to himself — at least in the area of juridical decisions — the full powers of his primacy. During a council the bishops themselves are *judices*, together with the pope; they are not simply advisors. They should not be and they have not been *judices* during these synods of bishops. They are only advisors, as was repeatedly made clear in these synods. But if this is the way things are, the ecclesiological problem remains unsolved, that is, whether the highest and universal fullness of power in the Church, which the Council attributed to the universal episcopate, can operate only in a council, or whether there are other ways as well in which these full powers might be active. If there are other ways, what would they look like in the concrete practice of the Church?

If this is impossible a priori, then in reality only the pope would be the bearer of the highest power in the Church, especially since only he can convene a council. This is one reason why the Council's doctrine about the body of bishops as subject of the supreme power in the Church is not easy to understand. We mentioned above that the synod of bishops has only an advisory function for the ruling of the Church by the pope, as indicated rather pointedly by the new Code of Canon Law. These synods of bishops may therefore be considered a modest contribution to a somewhat greater democratization. But one cannot appeal to them to clarify the meaning and realization of the Council's doctrine about the world episcopate.

Hence the Council proposes a theological task, which it does not carry out itself: to make it clear, in theory and practice, that the body of bishops directs the Church and how it does this. It is true that theoretically one may answer this question by saying that the college of bishops does it through the pope, who exercises his own full powers as head and as representative of the world episcopate. But this answer is not sufficient. For in practice it is not easy to see that the pope exercises his full powers precisely *as* head and as representative of the college of bishops. Yet he can exercise full power in this way, even though he does not receive his power from the college of bishops, since the latter does not exist without him. There is no need to show, by concrete examples, that Roman church leaders do not in practice make it clear that they exercise their power by virtue of a sort of feedback to the body of bishops. Yet we might say that such feedback is given by its very nature, although traditional ecclesiology does not clearly state it and the doctrine of the Council on the college of bishops teaches it only implicitly.

The Council's teaching about two somewhat distinct subjects of the highest power in the Church presents theology with a task for further reflection although theologians may be unable to come up with a solution that is absolutely clear. In the juridical field there are problems concerning the coexistence of rights that preclude the hope of a clear solution by means of a higher synthesis. (It seems to me, for instance, that the coexistence in a society of both unity and the need to delegate power is one such problem. It is impossible to solve it completely within a precise juridical framework. Outside the juridical domain we are referred to practice and history, to love and humility.) Yet the task is still there. Ecclesiology and canon law must first clearly explain the theoretical impossibility of solving the problem and draw the necessary conclusions. And for the domain of practice, they must examine how the significance of the college of bishops both within and outside of the papal government can come more fully into its own.

The pope could, for instance, at least *jure humano*, grant to the synod of bishops a *votum deliberativum*; canon law admits this possibility. Further, the powers of the individual bishop should be limited as little as possible. He leads the diocese in the name of Christ, not in the name of the pope. Thus it is possible to avoid the impression that individual bishops are merely regional deputies of the pope, whose mission and power are merely delegated to them by the pope.

There is no need to explain at length that the task thus entrusted to theology and canon law is of the highest ecumenical significance. It is enough to think of the problem of the appointment of bishops in the Church. The Church's nature does not demand that these appointments depend solely on the pope's free choice. They can also be made in some other way, under a particular law. The new code (can. 304, para. 1) admits this, although, typically, this admission has been inserted in the code almost as an afterthought.

THE UNIVERSALITY OF SALVATION

Another point that must be considered in connection with our theme, one which I no longer have to explain in detail,[1] is the hope that clearly emerged in the Council of a really universal salvation of the whole world and our ensuing new relationship to the other churches and communities, as well as to the non-Christian world religions. This hope of universal salvation explains why, in contrast to earlier times, the Council presumes good faith, a right moral attitude. It professes that grace is offered to all human beings, although not all of them accept it. This new worldview, which has become irreversible only with the Council, implies a great number of new theological suggestions that are evident and do not have to be explained in detail.

This universal hope is part of the folly of the cross that is expected from us, today's Christians. Despite all hope of progress, peace, and a better life, for a sober realist it is a hope against all hope (Rom. 4:18). In the long run it is the hope of eternal life — but for all. The Council encourages us to harbor this universal hope. Sober and realistic persons will find it hard to entertain such a hope, because every instance of progress they know of also means more dreadful violence and hopeless dying. But for us Christians this hope is obligatory. We are no longer allowed to hold in cold blood, as theoretically certain, like our Christian ancestors, that the definitive and permanent outcome of world history

[1]See Karl Rahner, *Concern for the Church: Theological Investigations 20*, trans. Edward Quinn (New York: Crossroad; London: Darton, Longman & Todd, 1981), pp. 97–102.

consists mostly in eternal damnation. This universal hope is also a burden. It is hard and we would betray it if we did not exert ourselves not to despair of our society and our history. Universal hope is a lasting gift from the Council; it is both a solace and a summons.

Does this not imply tasks that theology is still far from having carried out? When we keep in mind what the Council teaches about the universal salvific will of God at work everywhere, can grace still be conceived as circumscribed by space and time, as simply effected from without and from above, only given now and then — albeit always again — in a history that otherwise remains natural and profane? How must we interpret the dreadful evil in the world without belittling it, so that the doctrine of the universal, eschatologically irreversible, lasting, and effective salvific will of God does not remain just a verbal theorem, which is repeatedly being refuted by human malice?

How can there exist a real salvific faith in revelation where the verbal revelation of both Old and New Testaments has not penetrated? Is it still possible, in trying to answer this question, to appeal mythologically and naively to the primordial revelation in Paradise? We must now admit millions of years of salvation history, a long history of faith. Are we to explain it by assuming vaguely that the time elapsed between the beginning of humankind and Moses, a period of millions of years, has been taken care of by divine Providence, and without explaining how real revelation and faith in that revelation are possible? Is it enough to say with the Council that there are roads to salvation known only to God? How can we reconcile the absolute character of Christianity with the admission of a positive significance for salvation of non-Christian religions? Why can we, contrary to the trend that still prevailed under Pius XII, call non-Catholic communities "churches"? Exactly what does the Council mean when it says (*Lumen Gentium*, 8) that the Church of Jesus Christ is realized (*subsistit*) in the Roman Catholic Church, while avoiding an absolute identification that would be indicated by the word "is" (*esse*)? These and many other suggestions and questions that I cannot mention here are offered to us with this universal hope of salvation. That hope embraces all persons, all Christian communities, all non-Christian religions, so that it may gradually dawn on us how Christ has really died for all and how the Church is the universal sacrament of salvation for the whole world.

TASKS FOR SYSTEMATIC THEOLOGY

Here are a few more suggestions and questions that theology has not yet worked out. What theology of freedom stands behind the Declaration on Religious Freedom? What enormous theological tasks are presented to us by the Pastoral Constitution on the Church in the Modern World? What is implied by the fact that, contrary to the opinion of almost all theologians after the Council of Trent, the Council sees in the sacrament of penance a reconciliation with the Church as well? The Constitution on Divine Revelation tells us that the authors of Scripture are to be understood as truly independent authors, and not just persons who wrote what God dictated. How then shall we understand the inspiration of Scripture, the formation of the canon, and how we know about it? These and many other initiatives along the lines of dogmatic theology cannot be considered here. Today a certain weariness and resignation seems to have settled on systematic theology. This is certainly not due to the Council, which supplied theologians with many half-forgotten questions. These questions will have to be tackled bravely so that the proclamation of divine revelation by the Church today may be as it should and can be, and we may do our share so that God's word may be heard and God's grace be active and glorified.

10

PERSPECTIVES FOR PASTORAL THEOLOGY IN THE FUTURE

A PASTORAL STRATEGY FOR THE WORLD-CHURCH

What follows will contain a few considerations about the necessity of finding a strategy for pastoral theology that will be valid and workable for the world-Church. I do not believe, of course, that I can discover or develop such a plan, or even present it in this short article. I am convinced that such a pastoral strategy for the world-Church does not yet exist. So obviously I cannot develop it. But I hold that we should slowly begin to see that the time for such a global strategy in the Church has definitely come and is demanded by our times. We leave open the question *who* might develop it. Should it simply be the college of bishops with and under the pope, or the pastoral theologians of the world as they become aware of the problem, or a special Roman body to be organized for that purpose, or finally all of these agencies together?

When I say that the awareness of this task is hardly alive in the Church, I am not pronouncing a judgment on what takes place in the pastoral-theological consciousness of those who bear an immediate responsibility for the universal Church. Nor do I deny that there are tangible beginnings of this planning for a pastoral-theological strategy for the world-Church, as for instance in the works of Walbert Bühlmann. I mean only that it is not clearly present and tangible in existing institutions either in the Church at large or in Rome.

What I will say here is a timid attempt, whose only purpose is to contribute, to some extent, to awareness that the Church, in her pastoral theology and planning, has a duty to develop an explicit strategy for her pastoral task as a world-Church.

PASTORAL STRATEGY AND THE SYNOD OF BISHOPS

It might be said that the organization of the synod of bishops by Paul VI showed that such a duty had been recognized and undertaken. If this is true, I do not intend to underestimate the importance of these synods. But it seems to me that up to now the synod has considered what the individual local churches and their bishops have to do in carrying out their immediate duties for the present. I wonder whether in these synods of bishops the Church as *world*-Church, the Church as a *whole*, has explicitly pondered her pastoral strategy, as the strategy of the whole Church and as a strategy for the future. Even those who say "Yes" should not object to my present intent: to reflect on the need and the possibility of a pastoral strategy of the world-Church as such, and to hope that this planning, which did not and could not exist formerly, may have an appropriate subject. Should that subject be the college of bishops, or the synod of bishops, or a special Roman body set up for that purpose? This is a question of secondary importance, one that will easily be answered in theory and practice once the conviction is clearly alive in the Church's collective consciousness that today such a strategic pastoral plan is a necessity. Here then are a few ideas on the nature and need of such a plan.

PASTORAL STRATEGY AND
ROMAN CENTRAL GOVERNMENT

One more preliminary remark may be appropriate. One might think that the different bodies of the Church's Roman central government were taking care of this problem. There exists a Roman congregation for the evangelization of peoples (a general staff for the missions), a congregation for the oriental churches, one for the bishops, for the clergy, for the discipline of the sacraments and the liturgy, for religious and secular institutes, for education, and so on. There is a Secretariat of State. So, we might think that all these Roman bodies have some vision, that they do not worry only about what is to be done here and now but that in their inquiries and reflection they keep their eyes on the future. We might think that in this way all of them together would have a broad strategic plan for the pastoral tasks of the world-Church. Far be it from me to belittle these endeavors, if they exist.

Yet we might be slightly skeptical and wonder whether such a plan really is being developed in Rome. First, because in that case it would be a well-kept secret of the Roman central government. But should not the universal Church know of it, since it can be worked out in the right way only if the whole Church contributes her experience? Yet I do not believe that any member of the synod of bishops has ever heard of such a basic pastoral strategy for the world-Church. Moreover historically the Roman congregations were established and arranged in a random way, which was not modified by the reform of the curia under Paul VI. Can they be an effective and perceptive instrument for developing and carrying out such a plan? One might wonder whether, in their traditional aloofness from each other, the individual congregations are the right agency for such a common plan and its realization. The difficulties with regard to the respective jurisdictions of the Secretariat of State and the individual congregations and secretariats show that an ideal chain of authority and the ensuing collaboration, based on a single carefully worked out strategic plan, are still a desideratum. Finally even if all this had been nicely worked out in Rome, it would not be forbidden to lend a hand in this task.

As we reflect on the nature and the need of a strategic pastoral plan for the Church as a whole, we must not overlook two new facts that characterize the situation of the Church today. Together they make clear the possibility, nature, and necessity of such a pastoral plan for the world-Church, and they tell us who should develop and carry it out. Both the existence of a *world*-Church and the beginnings of a secular strategy for the future help us understand the nature and necessity of a strategic pastoral plan for the world-Church as such.

Today There Exists a World-Church

Christianity with its message of salvation was, of course, always destined for the whole of humankind and therefore potentially always a world-Church. But in fact neither as Judeo-Christian, nor as the Church of Roman-Christian culture and of the West, was the Church a world-Church in the actual sense of the word. And when, in the wake of European colonialism and imperialism in the sixteenth century, the Church started her expansion into the whole world and to all peoples, the result of her missionary activity was nothing more than Western Christianity exported throughout the world. The Church remained in fact an occidental Church with exports all over the globe. Today, as a result of the policies developed during the Second Vatican Council, the Church has really started to become a world-Church. Everywhere there are native bishops and clergy. The autonomy of the great regional churches was recognized in principle during the last Council. Everywhere, albeit with different intensity, initial moves are being made toward a theology that corresponds to the different cultures. Everywhere the inculturation of Christianity into the different cultures is, at least in principle, admitted as a duty of the Church. The former missionary churches are already starting, although quite timidly, to make their positive and active contribution to the life of the universal Church. Everywhere we notice difficulties and attempted solutions to the question of how to reconcile the unity of the Church with a lawful pluralism of the regional churches, so that the Church may really act and look like a world-Church.

The emergence of the Church as a world-Church is in fact, although not in its deepest nature, brought about by a newly emerging unity of humankind and by the ensuing development of global social activity and planning for this unified humankind. Formerly the fate and the history of individual peoples and groups were separated by a no man's land. At the time of Frederick William, the Great Elector (1620–88), the reality and history of Prussia were practically independent of the reality and history of Thailand. Today everything is interconnected. The life and destiny of every part of the earth are definitely and tangibly conditioned by whatever happens elsewhere in the world. That is why there have been world wars, which in former times were quite impossible. That is why there exists a United Nations and great superpowers with a global sphere of influence and power. Nowadays human history constitutes a unity; humanity is a unity not only on account of its origin, not only as an idea born in our heads, but as a directly tangible reality.

Humankind Begins to Plan Its Unity

At the same time, both as a result and a cause of this unity, humankind is planning its future and knows that such planning is a necessity. The future used to be considered the more or less unplanned and unconscious result of what befell people as a passively suffered natural fate and of what they themselves could do in their lifetime, without any desire or possibility of planning ahead. Today we are aware, or at least we are becoming aware, that the future is the realization of a *plan* for the future. In this way world and nature are not so much the available and natural places where people live but rather the material for a place to live, which people themselves plan and construct. That is why there are artificial substances that do not exist in nature, and why energies are tapped that are not of themselves available to humans, and so on.

Of course, this global planning of humanity's future is still in its infancy, because any kind of peaceful world government has still to be established. Such planning necessarily has its limits because, without mentioning other reasons, nobody would ever be able to assimilate all the data provided by a universal computer of rational world planning. Of course, this rational world planning entails enormous dangers for the self-destruction of humanity in the most diverse ways, which as we may notice, are already at work: atomic destruction, overpopulation with all its consequences, destruction of the indispensable requirements of human life, psychic dangers for humankind's global consciousness, of which we have hardly an inkling. But all of this does not change the fact that humankind is about to become a unified, active subject that plans and must plan for the future.

The idea that humanity might return to a more naive and spontaneous stage of consciousness and activity is a nostalgic utopia, whose realization would have to be paid for by the extinction of a great part of humankind. Humanity has reached the stage of conscious, rational self-planning; at least the beginning of this self-planning is evident. In the long run Marxist socialism may prove to be a fashion that will soon be outmoded. At the same time the individualism, which the West was able to afford with the restricted population of former times, is also a way of life of the past. Humankind therefore will have to look for newer and higher forms of socialization.

We can no longer do without global political planning, for which the United Nations is only a modest beginning. It aims at some kind of world government that, it is to be hoped, will not do away with the pluralism of peoples and cultures. One hundred years ago a neo-scholastic philosopher-jurist had already claimed that such a government was demanded by the natural law. It is probable that we will be practically unable and morally forbidden to control and modify human nature biogentically. But this does not mean that our biological existence will not and should not be planned and controlled — and not merely by curbing population growth. It stands to reason that in the future the management, increase, and protection of the prerequisites of human life in nature have to be rationally and globally planned. All these efforts at planning are but the first intimations that humanity's collective awareness is slowly entering the stage of a conscious planning for humankind itself.

It is precisely at this stage of human development, when humankind is slowly becoming the actively planning subject of its own self-realization, that the Church has at least begun to be a real world-Church. In the context of humanity's new theoretical and practical consciousness the Church too must plan for herself and her future in a new way.

PLAN AND FREEDOM

There is a need for an active global pastoral-planning strategy for the world-Church. Before trying to translate this thesis into more concrete language, I have to add a qualification which derives from the nature of human freedom, a freedom that is, of its very nature, never absolute. It is clear that humankind's active self-planning as a secular reality is never complete. The planners themselves are also the planned, and the future is always the coming of the unexpected. Even though we are supremely free, we have to do with available materials, which are never completely transparent.

As a result, in spite of all our planning, there are always unforeseen surprises. Moreover, by definition, freedom itself, time and again, upsets its own planning with unplanned decisions. A fortiori, all planning by the Church, every futurological approach to the Church, will in principle be an unfinished business. The Church must move into an unpredictable future. Indeed, the Church is the community of people who expect as their salvation that which cannot be planned, who accept as their everlasting bliss the incomprehensibility of God in the dawning of God's kingdom, who consider expectant waiting and watching for this incalculable future a fundamental duty of the Church. The Church in the world is the sacrament of the unplanned future because this future is the incomprehensibility of God himself.

However, this does not mean that human freedom and the Church's duty do not need any planning. We will be able to see the blessed heavens open above us when all we have built collapses on top of us. Nevertheless, we must always plan ahead and keep on trying to build a better dwelling place for ourselves. And the Church that is watching hopefully for the coming of God's incomprehensibility must also be a Church of social justice, of order, of missionary activity, of human rights, and also of human planning. In principle she has always been such. Today, however, she has to be all of these things as one *world*-Church, in the new context of a unified world, global human planning, and rational futurology.

DUTIES OF THE WORLD CHURCH

All of this means new problems ahead, which are hardly suspected as yet but which must be solved. For the solution of these problems the Church may have to look for wholly new, totally reorganized agencies. The following are a few comments about this. They do not claim to be systematic or to cover all aspects of the problem.

Building a New Awareness of the Faith

To mention a first example of a strategy for the world-Church, I believe that thorough reflection and planning are required with regard to the Church's consciousness, by which I mean the concrete awareness of the faith in the Church. The difference between what is officially taught as the faith of the Church and what is actually believed by the majority of the faithful has, for diverse reasons which cannot be analyzed here, become unbelievably greater than used to be the case. The Church should not and cannot manipulate collective consciousness, as happens in totalitarian states. Yet the connection required today between the official doctrine of the Church and the actual faith of the people can no longer be brought about through means that used to suffice for that purpose. The Congregation of the Faith as it is organized today, the encyclicals and allocutions of the pope in traditional vocabulary, the pastoral letters of bishops with their traditional accent and content, the usual preaching from the pulpit whose content is aimed at a few people and has little appeal to unbelievers and marginal Catholics, catechisms that continue to be as inbred as ever, all these are no longer adequate to bring the marvelous message of Christianity to people as they really are. They are unable to bridge the gap between the official faith of the Church and Christian doctrine as it really lives in the heads and hearts of Christians and in the more or less correct information of non-Catholics.

How should such a new shaping and erecting of the actual awareness of the faith be planned and organized? Who is to be entrusted with this task? The instruction of people through mere reliance on church authority keeps losing its efficacy. How can we change it into a formation that persuades through the inner splendor of the truth itself? I have no answer to all these questions. But they cannot be evaded, they must be answered within the framework of the Church's global strategy. The task involves a great diversity of theological problems. To solve them church leaders cannot passively wait for answers from theologians. They must actively cooperate, do their share, so that such questions may be clearly grasped and answered as well as possible.

Recently I asked why there was no papal encyclical about today's atheism. I continue to be amazed that papal encyclicals treat (correctly of course) the Incarnation of the eternal Word, without making the slightest attempt to render this fundamental doctrine of Christianity more accessible to today's unbelievers, to whom it sounds utterly absurd. (Recently a member of the Congregation of the Faith told me that the task of the magisterium was to see to it that Christian doctrine is not falsified or weakened, and that the positive interpretation and defense of this doctrine is the task of theologians.) That is not the way it should be today. Rather, the defense and interpretation of Christian doctrine by theologians should be encouraged and promoted by the magisterium. Eventually the latter should at least draw theologians' attention to the large number of questions that have been neglected. But it seems to me that the magisterium notices these questions even later than do theologians. Does, for instance, the frightening decrease in the frequency of confessions not involve a variety of theological questions, most of which both the magisterium and theologians simply ignore?

Here is a concrete point where, to my mind, what has just been said becomes clear. I suppose that in the old Church people knew what they had to believe upon hearing the Apostles' Creed (at least with a very short explanation). I suspect that, in spite of the normative significance that this creed has and will continue to have, people today understand little or nothing when they recite it, even if I try to explain it to them. They will ask me what they should understand by the word *God*, since, if God exists at all, he is certainly not living in the empyrean heaven and be still active two hundred million light years from us. Where can we find new, up-to-date, short formulations of the faith, by means of which today's unbelievers begin to *understand* what we Christians really believe?

A plan for systematic and pastoral theology should calmly and courageously head in the direction of a theology and proclamation that are open to the whole world. It is true that Christianity cannot deny in theory and practice its own historical origin. Everywhere in the world and in all its cultures it should always be clear that Christianity hails from Palestine and that it has passed through Western culture. But if and when Christianity is to become a world religion, that is, the religion of the peoples and cultures that did not originate near the Mediterranean or in the West, the only possible course is to be open to the whole world. This means that, in theory and practice, Christianity must become historically more neutral; it must let its historical origins, insofar as they do not affect its own nature, quietly fade away into history. We may ask what Christianity will look like when, in the non-Western world, its historical provenance has disappeared into a distant past, somewhat like the Jewish theology of Jesus' time that is no longer known to us and is of no interest. Such changes will certainly occur. But both systematic and pastoral theology should make it a policy to teach us to recognize the changes.

Universal Church and Particular Churches

Another important group of questions for a real global strategy of the Church refers to the still unsolved problem of the relation between the universal Church and the great regional churches. True, the Second Vatican Council solemnly declared that these churches are not simply administrative districts of the one universal Church, differing from each other only in a few small details. However, on the whole (if we overlook the small Uniate churches of the Near East) nothing has come of this general principle. Rome continues to look for the most uniform canon law possible. For example, the approved liturgies are in fact nothing but translations of the Roman liturgy.

Of course, some may claim that the Church's unity renders such uniformity necessary in the universal Church. But by holding such a position, they can easily sabotage the principle of the relative independence and diversity of the great regional churches and reduce the principle to mere lip service. What degree of autonomy, what tangible initiatives has Rome really granted to the churches of South America or of Indonesia? Of course in practice it is not easy to work out the consequences of the dialectical relationship between universal and particular churches. But where is the authority that, together with the universal Church, courageously thinks these problems through and sees to it that these consequences are realized?

The World Responsibility of the Church

In the Second Vatican Council the Church loudly and expressly proclaimed her global responsibility, her responsibility for peace and justice in the world. During the past few decades she has certainly done much in this regard, although much of what has been said and done by the highest authority in the Church has afterward been sabotaged by the indolence or quiet resistance of subordinates. Would it not be possible for the Christian churches to think of even more steps, especially more concrete ones, in this regard? Does the Church today have the courage to come up with more concrete demands for social change, for peace and disarmament, even when they are rejected within the Church herself, especially by politicians? Is there an agency in Rome that really studies all these questions systematically and accurately (and not just because of some official's praiseworthy good will) and, with real courage, strives for concrete solutions? Naturally there are those in Rome who busy themselves with such problems, who represent the Holy See at various congresses and meetings. But it is difficult for the average Christian to find a single courageous voice in Rome speaking on behalf of the Church's global responsibility. Indeed, it looks as if in Rome, despite the pope's world travels, the courage for such tasks is decreasing, not increasing. It seems that Rome is anxious and nervous, preferring to call back to the sacristy those Christians who are actively trying to carry out their task of social criticism in the world.

The Diaspora Situation of Christians

It seems to me that this elusive topic of a global pastoral strategy for the world-Church has a further task, in addition to the many others that will not be mentioned here. I would like to call this task the problem of the Church's diaspora situation. For all practical purposes the Church acts on the unstated presupposition that there still exists a more or less intact homogeneous Catholic Christianity, as was the case until well into the twentieth century, and as may still be the case in Poland today. For instance, it was taken for granted that Catholics married Catholics. A mixed marriage could be treated as an unusual exception, which was patiently and cautiously tolerated. It was easy to organize Catholic social organizations, to press for Catholic schools, and to keep artistic, literary, and leisure activities mostly within the Church, under Catholic auspices.

Today this situation is practically finished. Christians live so much in the diaspora that, even in groups controlled by the Church, committed and fervent Catholics are often only a small majority. Although this situation exists in traditionally Christian countries as well as in the so-called missions, it seems to me that it has not yet led the Church to really systematic and courageous theological and pastoral reflection. Everywhere Catholics of the diaspora speak the language of their environment, a secular language. All of this being the case, what religious language can the Church use to make itself understood? What do people today take for granted in their personal lives? Could these questions be the starting point for attempts to make Christianity understandable and believable? The ancient Church tolerated a moral doctrine that included slavery as practiced by the general population. What opinions are "taken for granted" today, although in fact they may be morally questionable or false? Might not the Church quietly, but this time with full awareness, ignore this without wasting its energy in unsuccessful protests?

Can the Church today simply continue to presume as she used to do that outside, and even within, the Church all so-called marriages start with the intention that is required for a really indissoluble marriage? As the Church endeavors to promote morality, should she not more carefully and more impartially take into account the social and political presuppositions of the different cultures than she did formerly, when Western Christian morality was simply exported to mission countries? Recently a bishop from South America asked how useful it was for the Church naively to sing the praise of marriage in a country where the majority of children are born out of wedlock. On what specific fronts of the campaign for morality (and not on all of them at once) should the Church fight resolutely in order to witness in the world to the grandeur and dignity of Christian morality?

Today, as was always the case, Christian morality emphasizes certain points without thereby rescinding or denying other principles. Would it not make more sense to a secularized world if the rejection of the arms race that is becoming more and more insane were a more important characteristic of Christianity than the rejection of artificial contraception? Such shifts in what morality emphasizes have always occurred. (During the reign of Louis XIV the popes did not lose any sleep because of that king's immoral war policy, and who will blame them for it?) But today such shifts in emphasis should be considered in a global pastoral strategy. If the Church does not simply look perfunctorily at this diaspora situation and forget about it, she has to make a choice. Is she going to try by all means possible to hold on to the policy of spreading out pastoral care everywhere as uniformly as possible. Or should she try to develop, somewhat like oases in the desert of our secularized world, instances of pastoral ministry, even if this means the end of a uniformly thin and not very attractive presence? Whatever the solution the universal diaspora situation has confronted our global pastoral strategy with tasks that are far from being sufficiently recognized and fulfilled.

Turning Away from a Bourgeois Church

Today we often talk about turning away from a bourgeois Christianity, from a service Church. What is right in such a demand? What can be done about it today? What is better left for the future? What have we rightly taken over, and what perhaps not so rightly, from other countries and cultures? What is so utopian that it cannot be realized in the future as our secularized society continues to develop? It is, of course, impossible to answer all these questions here.

Yet the demand to turn away from a bourgeois Church includes an important and correct view of the future, which we have to think about and plan for. If, for instance, the Church really wants to hold on to celibacy in the future, this position will entail far-reaching changes. Today's church leaders do not clearly see them and intend them even less, yet changes will inexorably come if the Church is not to shrink into an insignificant sect.

Lay people will necessarily enjoy more independence, power, and importance. In base Christian communities they will, to a large extent, do the work of the Church. As ordinary Christians we will firmly expect that the Church of the future will continue to be the Church of the ancient Christian faith, with that organization which her present faith declares to belong to divine and immutable right.

Nonetheless, in the year 2200 the Church in her visible features will look quite different from what we are used to. Is this transformation of the Church something unwanted and unforeseen but that will happen anyway? Is it going to "happen" gradually without much foresight, imposed upon her piecemeal by the present situation, in the way in which the Church of medieval feudalism followed upon the Church of the Fathers? Or, given the present condition of collective human consciousness, should it not also be — although not primarily — a duty of the Church to foresee and, as much as possible, to *plan* in advance this coming transformation of the Church? Should there not exist in the Church a global pastoral strategy that looks to the future more than has been the case up to now? And is this not possible? To my mind this is a real problem for the Church of today, which has not yet received sufficient attention.

11

THE FUTURE OF CHRISTIAN COMMUNITIES

Something must be said about the future of the Christian communities that, for all practical purposes, are identified with our parishes. No prophecies are to be made for the next five years; we have to look further ahead into the future. So we have to start from a point that is quite different from what might at first be expected. That is why we ask the reader to be patient.

Christianity has been in existence for two thousand years. Yet the greater part of humanity has not really come under the Church's influence, and so is not yet Christian. If I ask Christians whether we should send missionaries to try to convert these peoples, really good Christians will say, "of course." They will say: "Even if these people who are not Christians are to be saved through the hidden grace of God in a manner that, as the Council says, is known only to God, and provided they have not decisively and definitively acted against their conscience, even then all human beings should become Christians." And they are quite right. But still the question remains how God, in his Providence, after two thousand years, can allow the greater part of humanity to still be living outside Christianity. God must have a reason for this strange fact. While we can say that these reasons are hidden in the unfathomable will of God and should therefore be adored in silent submission, we can still give them some thought.

A CHRISTIAN WORLD?

Let us suppose for a moment that Christianity has spread all over the world. Everywhere there exist only Christian peoples. Even public opinion is Christian. Everywhere there are churches and bishops that are held in high esteem; the pope is welcomed all over the world with great enthusiasm. Even then the situation of each individual person would still be that of a mysterious radical struggle between light and darkness, between God and evil, between the option for God and eternal life and the option for definitive perdition. In other words, in spite of all the appearances of Christianity, the world would still be one in which darkness and light struggle with each other in a fight whose outcome we cannot predict according to merely human criteria.

If God lets individuals live to the end of their lives in a struggle between good and evil, we must also apply this to ordinary history. According to God's will this struggle must be manifest in a social manner; it cannot remain hidden in the interiority of the individual. So even supposing that one day all of humanity were externally christianized in a certain sense, things would not be very different. In the public eye there would still persist anti-Christian powers; in history, in politics, and in the arts, a lasting struggle would still go on for and against Christ. That is the way God seems to have willed it: God wants humanity to make free decisions, and not merely in each individual's interiority, but in the full view of history.

If we assume this view (although we cannot foresee exactly what it would look like in a humanity that, to all appearances, would everywhere be Christian), we understand at once that in such a situation real Christians would continue to be a minority. Even in such an ideal future, one which popes and bishops may have in mind and long for, real Christians would still be an embattled segment of humankind; they would, as we said, be challenged, opposed, and fought against, not only in the intimacy of each one's moral decision making, but also in the public eye. In other words true Christians cannot seriously expect to live in a uniformly Christian world.

OASES IN A NON-CHRISTIAN WORLD

Let us presuppose all this and ask ourselves how one should envisage the near future of a Christian community. First, it is not certain that in our so-called Christian Europe there will ever be communities that completely cover the whole territory of a country or state. This statement does not proclaim an ideal for the future; it simply makes a sober realistic conjecture about how things will look in reality. There will be too few priests. Of course, we can hope that the number of priests starts growing again, but in a population in which only 10 to 15 percent of the people are actually "practicing" Catholics, we cannot expect that this small percentage will provide so many priests that the other 85 percent will be provided for. So we will have communities that will constitute a minority of the total population. For a realist, it is not probable that European secularized society will in the foreseeable future become Christian again, explicitly and in practice. In other words, we will have small communities with few priests. Thus, in the long run, it will probably not be possible for these communities with their few priests to reach immediately and directly, like police precincts, the whole population, the dechristianized.

It seems to me that, as a result, future communities, as well as so-called parishes, will no longer be able to feel responsible administratively for the total population of a country, as they have up to the present. Today, if we ask a pastor, "How many people are in your parish?" he will say, for instance, "ten thousand." By this he means that perhaps 1,500 of them are practicing Christians but that he also feels immediately responsible for the 8,500 others. It will be impossible for this to go on in the foreseeable future. It is not un-Christian and un-Catholic to expect that in the near future (in a matter of decades) Christian communities will be somewhat like oases in a non-Christian world. Communities of the future should, of course, not withdraw into a shell or a ghetto. They should be thoroughly missionary. They will have to present Christianity in a really attractive way. (We will have to come back to this point.) But these separate communities should not feel as though they were pitiful remnants of a larger community to which many more, five times more, people ought to belong. The same also applies to pastors, spiritual leaders, and all who direct such a community.

Once one gets rid of the idea (not out of pessimism or laziness, but in a sober analysis of the situation of Christians in today's Western world) that the Christian parish community must be so organized and administered that it extends all the way to the neighboring parish and that all the members of these parishes should be equal to the total population, one has a picture of the situation in our country that can be expected for the Church in the world at large. Everywhere else in the world there are regions in which Christianity, whether Catholic or not, constitutes only minorities, only isolated oases. So when this situation carries over to Europe, and when the appearance of a universal, public christianization of Europe vanishes, one has only to be concerned with what in principle is to be expected from the Church's nature and from human freedom. We say this in consideration of the Church's situation in the world and in the public eye.

SO THAT GOD'S SALVATION MAY BECOME VISIBLE

One can really say to each community what the Second Vatican Council said about the self-understanding of the universal Church as present in the world: The Church is the sacrament of universal salvation. What does this mean? She is a historically tangible sign, willed by God, a sign that God loves the world as a whole, that he does not release it from the grip of his powerful love, and that he intends to lead it to its blessed consummation in ways that are not known to us. The Church is the great sacramental sign of all these things. But a sign is never simply identical with what it signifies. Therefore, while the Church is the sacramental *sign* of the world's salvation, we know that salvation extends far beyond it.

We can also apply this conception of the nature of the Church to a particular community, as it is now, or as it shows signs of becoming. Such a community is an oasis in a world that is secretly always filled with God's grace but that, seen from without, socially, looks very unholy, very pagan. The community is the visible sign of salvation that God has established in this seemingly godless world. Through this community God says: I am here in this world and I remain with my grace; secretly I fill the deepest depths of humanity, keeping people in the love that I, the eternal God, have for my only-begotten Son, the Incarnate Word. Of this, each Christian community is the sacramental sign for its environment. The sign is different from what it signifies, namely the quiet, hidden salvific will of God in the whole secular world. God desired a sign because, as the God of the Incarnation, as the God become visible, he wanted not only to be the deepest hidden life of the world but also to let his universal love become manifest in history. God desired this to happen in such a way that the salvation which God proffers to the whole world might become visible in its ultimate Christian explicitness.

At this point a Christian might say: If that is true, I myself might make my life easier. I am going over to the world, which, according to what we have just said, is not living outside of God's salvific will, which can attain its salvation even outside the visible Church. I will therefore forego explicit Christianity with all the obligations that go with it: Sunday Mass, receiving the sacraments, being controlled by church authorities, and so on.

Christians, however, may not speak this way. Why? Because they have come under the influence of God's grace in Jesus Christ and in the Church, unlike many others, even though we cannot draw an exact boundary between the two. But those Christians who have expressly encountered Jesus Christ and his Church cannot say: I look for my salvation *outside* explicit Christianity, which refers to and believes in Jesus Christ and his Church, with her sacraments, and so on. Should they speak that way, after having been specially chosen by God, they would be rejecting their very salvation. In other words: This conception of an oasis-like Christian community, as a sacramental sign of salvation for the world around it by no means implies that Christians would be allowed to break away, as it were, from this sign to which they belong in order to join anonymous Christianity, for which God's salvific will is at work mysteriously — albeit always on account of Christ.

MADE FREE FOR A MISSIONARY TASK

It is time to show that, for reasons derived from the nature of Christianity, the community understood as an oasis will not be surprised that, although only a minority, it stands under order to engage in missionary activity. And the community will understand that, by accepting this minority status, it can accomplish so much more naturally and freely. First, it is clear that this community, as a sign of salvation for others, must take care that the sign does not perish. The visible and tangible presence of the world's salvation, related to Jesus Christ and called Church, must be present in the world until the end of time. We cannot determine how large and powerful this sign is in proportion to the totality of humankind, but it must by all means continue to exist.

Those who know that they have been called to this explicit form of salvation as a sign for others and who therefore cannot ignore their social responsibility, their love for neighbor, must see to it that this community remains alive, that it continues to grow, and that it gains new members from the surrounding secular society. Those who have been taken over by God's grace, not in a wordless anonymous way, that is not without awareness of their privilege, those who know that they really are God's beloved children and who realize that they have been called to an everlasting life in God's immediacy, should also make this privilege known to others. They are aware of the blessing that has come to them. Let them therefore tell others about it so that this sign of the world's salvation that is called Church may keep radiating from them ever more intensely, so that it may win over more people and fill them with the awareness of this innermost blessing of grace.

A community that does not continually lament because only 15 percent of its members are practicing Catholics, but rather rejoices because of those who are active, has a better chance of being filled with missionary zeal than a community in which, like a cancerous growth, the depressing feeling prevails that it is really not what it ought to be, because 85 percent of its members have turned away. The former, impelled by what it knows about itself from faith, is the sacramental sign of salvation for those who do not yet properly and actively belong to it; it can be filled with a much less biased and more lively missionary zeal.

THE TASK OF THE PRIEST

Some time ago I said that a priest or a bishop should be asked how many *new* Christians he had gained in his so-called Christian, but in reality un-Christian, territory. He should attach more importance to this than to the question of how many "still" belong to his community or his diocese. This question also allows us to understand the proper task of a priest as community leader in the parish of the future. Through his existence, his deeds, and his words, he is, as it were, the living, believing, hoping, loving witness of God's message. That is why he tries to win over at least a few followers.

It is from the characteristics of a spiritual guru (if I may speak this way) that a priest of the future should get an idea of his function. He is not first and foremost the one who must see to it that all those who in fact do not know what it really means receive baptism, be married in the church, and be buried from the church. He is not the one who should in a precise way find out what percentage of his so-called parishioners actually fulfill their Easter duty. Rather, he is one who is filled with a salutary faith in Jesus Christ crucified and risen from the dead. Aware of the fact that he has been freed and redeemed, he is impelled by his faith in life eternal to share with as many people as possible (how many is unimportant) his own experience of redemption and liberation. He would, of course, also share the faith by means of the sacraments, especially the celebration of the Lord's Supper. But all of this must be included in the proclamation of the liberating, redeeming, and saving grace of God.

Such a pastor will feel at ease in a so-called base Christian community. I cannot discuss here the extent to which such base Christian communities should in the future coincide with parish communities. It is quite possible that even in a wonderfully active parish community there may still, or perhaps even there should still, exist base communities, as parts of such a parish. In any case, because of the powerful influence of such a pastor, the parish community itself should become a base community.

BASE CHRISTIAN COMMUNITIES AND CHANGES

Persons who share a profound love of God should also share other concerns, and the love that the Holy Spirit inspires for God and neighbor should practically and concretely become manifest in a true community of mutual love and service. The priest, inspired by such true Christian fervor, feels naturally drawn to such a base community, his parish. And such a parish is a missionary parish. Trusting in God, it is not upset by the fact of being only a small minority in the great wide world, because it is a minority that promises and that actually brings God's salvation to the world at large.

This allows us to answer a number of other questions. First, such a base community, with their priest (we might almost call him their "spiritual father"), will be interested in ecumenical work. Its members are those who have come under the mighty spell of God (we might almost call them, by God's grace, mystics of daily life), and they want to live like brothers and sisters. In such a community differences among churches are not, to be sure, simply ignored (this would lead to a third confession), but its genuine Christian spirit renders those differences less important, so that there is hope that they may be overcome. Should a pastor use a chasuble at Mass, or simply a gown like a minister? Should we make frequent pilgrimages to Rome, or should our reverence for the Petrine office be more reserved, as befits its position in the hierarchy of Christian truths? For such questions, these base charismatic communities may well supply an answer that leads to real church unity.

In such a base community the relationship between priests and lay people undergoes a change. Not in the sense that there should be no more priests in the Church, and not in the sense that in a community needing some kind of organization there would not be different functions and tasks, whose distribution would be accepted by all with respect and love. But in such a community there is a function for *everyone*. In addition to the function of leading the community, especially at the Lord's Supper, there are many other indispensable functions. The pastor's function would, of course, not be limited to ritual. As community leader, he should feel a responsibility to be, through his whole life, a living and powerful example of Christian life for his brothers and sisters. There will, nevertheless, always remain some difference between an official function in such a community and the real meaning of the community.

THE EXAMPLE OF A CHESS CLUB

I will try to explain this first by means of an example, although that example has often been attacked (for instance by Gisbert Greshake). The main purpose of a chess club is to see to it that its members are good, even outstanding, chess players. That is the purpose and the meaning of a chess club. Yet such a club needs a president, a treasurer, and other officers who arrange everything so that good chess may be played. It is desirable for the president to know something about chess, even to be a very good chess player. That helps him or her understand better how a chess club should be organized. But it is also quite possible that the president is not the best player, that other members are better players.

Something similar happens in the Church. The saints are the best chess players in the chess club of God's Church. Her leaders too, that is, the pope and the bishops, should, of course, be as holy as possible. But nobody can take it amiss (nor has this ever happened in the Church) if they are not as holy, as radically Christian, as powerfully influential for the good as the Church's great saints. I should not call for the resignation of the club president because he or she lost a game with one of the members. Likewise, we cannot demand too much from the leaders of the Church as a "society," as if, in order to be leaders, they had to be the best Christians. A bishop may at times stand spiritually lower than his chauffeur, who is a humble and unselfish Christian, foregoing more lucrative employment to work for his bishop as a service to the Church. It does not follow that the chauffeur should take over the bishop's function. On the other hand, priests, pastors, bishops, and religious, who have specific functions and tasks in the Church, must often remind themselves that, in the long run, they can carry them out in the right way only if they endeavor to be radically Christian.

NEW FUNCTIONS IN THE CHURCH

The Church has a social organization which, she is convinced, is part of her nature. She is convinced that there will be deacons, priests, and bishops in the Church in the future, as there are today. But two points remain undecided.

First, it is not clear what exactly the task of these three hierarchic functions should be in a given historical and social setting. Possibly, as Franz Xaver Kaufmann has pointed out, a Church of the future would have much smaller dioceses, because more than in the past their vitality will depend on the vitality of their leaders. In the course of history priests have assumed many tasks that do not necessarily belong to their function of presiding at the eucharistic celebration, tasks they have given up at other times. Deacons, priests, and bishops will not necessarily have the same functions in the future as they had in the past.

In the second place, this permanent hierarchic structure of the Church does not mean that all the functions that she has to fulfill as Church belong necessarily to members of the hierarchy. Where, for instance, does the hierarchical structure indicate the need for teachers in the Church? We might say, of course, that the bishop is the official teacher within his diocese. But this does not exclude the possibility, or even the necessity, of specially appointed teachers outside the hierarchic structure. There might also be a special function of official church charity. The Church must practice charity, not only in her members as they take care of the poor, but also as Church. So there could be a function like that of the deacons mentioned in the Acts of the Apostles (6:2ff.). It is not certain that this task can be carried out as it should by priests, pastors, directors of Catholic Charities, or the permanent deacons who are now being ordained. There might also be a function of social criticism that would call attention to social grievances, or a function of explicitly Catholic education or psychotherapy, and so on. All these examples should only make it clear that, besides the three traditional functions mentioned above, there could also exist in the Church other official tasks, which would deserve respect and a certain autonomy. These tasks and functions should not depend on the arbitrary power of the pastor or of the individual bishop. Rather, they should be accepted by the hierarchy as present-day specializations of the one all-embracing function of the Church as required by today's circumstances.

This does not mean that individual laypersons and groups of laypeople would not be important in the Church. The Church does not live only, and certainly not principally, in the hierarchy and its different members. As People of God on its pilgrimage through history, she lives in all her members. And wherever Christians, impelled by their faith, perform their Christian duties in family or society, there the Church lives and there she may have more of an impact than she has through the hierarchy. In the past holy kings did not live in vain. Saints can be found outside the silence of cloistered monasteries. For example, Saint Teresa of Avila regretted that in her time women had so little influence. It is as a missionary for the salvation of the world that Saint Thérèse of Lisieux chose to be a contemplative Carmelite nun, because, as she said, for her there was no other way of doing it. Wherever they are, as members of the Church Christians have a duty to influence the Church as well as the world and public opinion.

TEMPORARY PRIESTS

Many more questions might be brought up about minor points. For instance, without going against the sacramental character of the priesthood, could the Church not admit an easier way for persons to resign from the priestly life, one that does not morally disqualify the person in question? We might wonder, of course, whether allowing some kind of temporary priesthood might not have an adverse psychological and social influence on the priesthood. This is a question that requires reflection and perhaps some experimentation. But, theoretically speaking, I do not believe that the so-called lasting character of the priesthood, which according to the Council of Trent can never be lost, would dogmatically make priesthood for a time absolutely impossible. The Church does indeed laicize priests, and it is not clear why in the eyes of the Church the grounds for laicization can only consist in some moral lapse. The question comes up then whether a correctly conceived temporary priesthood might not attract more young men who are afraid of assuming the priesthood because they are not sure they can shoulder a commitment for life.

THE ORDINATION OF WOMEN

Moreover, in my humble opinion, the question remains open whether, in a social and, we might say, anthropological setting that differs considerably from our present male-dominated one, the ordination of women is dogmatically impossible. True, the Congregation of the Faith has declared that it is. Therefore, realistically, we need not expect that in the foreseeable future the Church will withdraw this opinion and take the consequences. This declaration of the Congregation of the Faith is not an infallible dogma; it stands in history and might eventually be revised.

The Church's teaching authority has revised and practically withdrawn much more fundamental declarations. To take an example at random: The declaration made by the Biblical Commission under Pius X stating that Moses is, quite literally, the author of the whole Pentateuch was intended to have at least the same authority as the one claiming that women cannot be ordained. Yet after sixty years this declaration has become obsolete and without authority. Could the same thing happen in the present case? Will it happen? How long will it take before it happens? It is impossible to answer these questions. There are undoubtedly many people in North America and also to some extent in Europe who consider it discriminatory against women that they cannot be ordained.

Yet we should not exaggerate. Returning to our chess club we might say, metaphorically: It is much more important for women to be good chess players, that is, to live the Christian life as radically as possible, to live Christianity as the religion of Jesus Christ, the crucified and risen one, as the religion of freedom and of love. This is something that nobody forbids them to do. This matters much more than — in the chess club again — being a pastor or a priest or a bishop in the Church. When we keep in mind the main purpose of Christianity, the question of admissibility to a function in the Church's social dimension is secondary, compared with the question of how a woman today can be autonomous and emancipated and, at the same time, live Christianity as a woman.

THE FARTHEST BECOME THE NEAREST

Today humankind has become a single global entity in the world. Each one's fate depends on all the others. The different groups and nations are no longer separated by historically empty intervals. What happens in Latin America in the next fifty years will influence what happens in Europe, and the other way round. Even the most remote peoples have now become the nearest. A thousand years ago, if we overlook the Turkish danger, what happened in India or East Asia was a matter of indifference to Christians in Europe. Europeans were unable to influence the situation in these countries, and the command of Christian charity had little meaning for their abstract relationship to these peoples. Today the situation is totally different. Ecological concerns, international peace, development of

Third World countries, and so on, are the responsibility of every Christian and of every Christian community.

In our time a parish must have an effective relationship with a parish in Nigeria. Problems of disarmament, of peace all over the world, of aid to the Third World, problems that today's so-called Greens bring up (although often in a very emotional and naive way) are problems that must become the responsibility of individual Christians and Christian communities. It is not clear how much individuals can do in this respect. Yet can they do nothing? While that might be true for beggars on the street (and even they can pray for the Third World), ordinary Christians can at least see to it that their representatives in larger social organizations, for instance in political parties and in the State, carry out their obligations and responsibilities with regard to these problems.

How many Christians have protested to their parties, because less than one percent of the gross national product is devoted to the Third World? How many Christians have made it known to their parties that they are willing to give up one percent of their salary for the Third World? In Berlin there are a few university professors who give up a considerable amount of their salary, so that the State, in its eagerness for savings, will not abolish a certain number of academic chairs. A famous educator who is already retired told me that she would honestly have to admit that she could live quite well if her pension were 10 percent less than it is, and that she was willing to take such a cut. If West Germany had civil servants who were willing to take a cut of a few percentage points in their salaries, a great amount of poverty would disappear. Why are there so few Christians who are ready to do something of the kind, and who do not hide this readiness in their heart but make it publicly known? Such things should be considered more openly and critically, with a greater readiness for change, than is the case at present.

A COMMUNITY OF PRAYER

A Christian community should not be a service station, where people come just to satisfy their individual need for piety and salvation. Such a community also has political and social obligations that should be clearly mentioned from the pulpit. (On the other hand, a priest who is mostly concerned with social and political topics should also speak of God, eternal life, faith in and hope of eternity.) However, a truly Christian community should not be just a social or political group, working for justice in the world. It must also be a community that looks to God in worship and prayer.

A community that is no longer attuned to common prayer, to a kind of prayer that is not simply a legalistic fulfillment of an obligation but really prayer in spirit and in truth, prayer that soars beyond all earthly goods to be a prayer of radical hope in the eternal life of God — such a community is no longer a Christian community. There are prayer meetings and services that may and even should have a more private character than the parish liturgy. But even the liturgy should be planned in such a way, with a kind of creative imagination and feeling of religious intimacy, that people can pray personally and fervently and can lift their whole hearts in praise of God in song.

12

RITES CONTROVERSY: NEW TASKS FOR THE CHURCH

T here is at present no controversy over rites, such as the Church endured a few centuries ago, and which was settled only under Pius XI. The enculturation of Christianity and church life in foreign cultures is no longer bound by rigid rules, called useful and necessary by some and totally un-Christian by others. In that original sense there is no more rites controversy today. Yet the real problems behind it are becoming more urgent than ever.

For two reasons. First, Christianity has become a world religion, the Church has really started to be a world-Church. That is why the question of how to make Christianity and the Church acceptable in all cultural milieux has become an urgent question everywhere. There is a second reason too. Until the middle of the twentieth century the West European and North American cultures were predominant in the world, and they considered it their duty to impose their lifestyles as a blessing all over the world. Today this cultural predominance of the West has vanished. There is no doubt that formerly even the Church's missionaries were to a great extent imbued with this idea. Today the superiority of the European style of life has become questionable, and the problem of the enculturation of Christianity in other countries and societies more difficult.

NO SYNTHESIS

The question first emerged clearly in Matteo Ricci's time. Earlier, for instance, when the Church moved from the Roman to the Germanic culture, it was not so urgent. Today it is more urgent than ever and it points to a fundamental task of the Church. We may believe, as some church pronouncements still believe, that if we dropped or slightly modified some peculiarities generally used in organizing our Christian life or formulating our faith, we would more or less automatically enculturate Christianity in other peoples. There is no need to build gothic churches in China or Japan, or to introduce in these countries the kind of music we use in Europe. The task is quite simple and easy.

I for one believe that it is very, very difficult. Of course, some adaptations must be made, perhaps much more than in the past. But even as the differences between two individuals may be so great that no higher idea or synthesis can bridge them, so there are individual cultures that cannot come to understand each other simply by making a few practical adjustments and adaptations. It is in fact a profound theological problem whether one and the same Church can exist in different cultural milieux. We Christians are convinced that it can.

The Church must have a visible unity in worship, law, and faith. But how to achieve this unity while respecting the profound differences among cultures remains an unsolved problem. At present we expect and admit a pluralism in theologies. Although Rome, of course, keeps putting on the brakes, we admit in principle the possibility, and even the necessity, of great regional churches, with different liturgies and even, despite a basic unity in canon law, with very great differences in the laws of these churches.

The new Code of Canon Law applies only to the Latin Church. But if we overlook the Eastern churches of the Near East, this Latin Church coincides in fact with the Roman Catholic Church of the West, which has spread all over the earth. The trouble is that it is not clear yet whether church leaders sufficiently trust the regional churches to let them develop in their own way. The real rites controversy is still ahead of us. What will the Africans, with their way of understanding marriage, family, and tribal feeling, do with our European moral teachings? To what extent can these moral teachings be transplanted into other cultures? How will religious life look in East Asia, if we allow the Asians to follow their own ways. There can be no doubt that religious life, religious garb, and maybe even the liturgy will look quite different from the way they look today. All this will not be merely a slightly adapted translation of *our* Christianity, but something quite different. On the other hand, the whole of Christianity must continue to derive from the concrete historical Jesus, and we must maintain the unity of the Church in a real and practical way. There will, of course, always be a pope, although we might wonder with Bühlmann whether it would not be better for him to have his diocese in the Philippines.[1]

NEW TASKS

There is no need to consider this new universal rites controversy as something distasteful. It is a task that devolves upon the whole Church. And here the courage, the confidence, the optimism, and the openmindedness with which Matteo Ricci viewed foreign cultures can continue to serve as an example. First steps have already been taken. The decrees on the Eastern Church acknowledge that a real autonomy and diversity of the regional churches are a positive characteristic of the Church. It is not a Catholic ideal to render the Church so uniform, so homogeneous, that it is made up merely of regionally different branches of one universal church administration. The same problem exists for ecumenism. We should not aim at a Church in which the Latin Roman Catholic Church swallows up the other Christian churches and becomes the Church of all Christians without any inner change, merely through a quantitative increase in members. If the ecumenical question can be solved at all, it will happen only if we grant to the other great Christian churches the right to be *partner* churches in the one Catholic Church.

Within the Roman Catholic Church we have already experienced a relatively intense pluralism. Thus the Latin American Church is developing a theology of liberation that probably cannot simply be

---

[1]See W. Bühlmann, *Wenn Gott zu allen Menschen geht: Für eine neue Erfahrung der Auserwählten* (Basel, 1981), *Wo der Glaube lebt: Einblicke in die Lage der Weltkirche* (Freiburg i. Br., 1974), and *All Have the Same God* (Slough, U.K.: St. Paul Publications, 1988).

adopted by us. In Germany and in Western Europe there is a great diversity of theological trends.

UNITY IN CHRIST

Pope Paul VI told me once that theological pluralism should not turn into anarchy. That is quite true. But where does a lawful pluralism start, and how do we distinguish it from an anarchistic pluralism? When that question is asked in concrete cases, it often remains unanswered. Africans too will want to develop an African theology. The question will be how it can be their own while remaining a lawful theology within the one Church. We should probably admit that very often these different theologies cannot quite understand each other. For if they did, we would once more have a synthesis of several theologies, and there would be no more pluralism. In canon law, in theology, in liturgy, and so on, there should prevail in the Church a tolerance which allows everyone to tell the other: I do not quite understand everything you say, and yet you are my brother or sister in the one Church.

I believe that the Church will have to do some rehearsing for this tolerance of different opinions which we do not quite understand. The present attitude seems to be somewhat as follows: What I do not understand in the other, what does not *positively* agree with what I have in mind, cannot be acceptable in the Church. And that is wrong. If we wonder how these theologies that we cannot reconcile with our own can exist in the one Church with her one faith, I would say: We are one because we are all baptized, because we all look on Jesus as the mediator of our salvation. And we are also one because we remain legally and liturgically in communion with one another. This framework provides a unity that enables us to bear and to respect a plurality of opinions. An encounter between two human beings never overcomes an ultimate residue that is unfamiliar and not understandable. Should they perfectly understand each other, they would in fact have become one and the same person. Not only would that be most unreal, it would not be at all interesting. Human beings are such that they accept the other person *as* one whom they do not understand perfectly, *as* unfamiliar, *as* the one who, to some extent, seems strange. This must also be recognized and accepted in the Church.

LIMITS OF TOLERANCE

But there is also an anarchistic pluralism. When a regional Church, the Church of a given cultural milieu or theology, entrenches and isolates itself, when it solemnly declares that it has nothing to learn from another Church — at that moment the love which tolerates pluralism without giving up unity would vanished. Gone would be the resolve to adhere to the truth of God's universal revelation. So this kind of disunity cannot be accepted.

In the sixteenth, seventeenth, and eighteenth centuries the Jesuits and the Dominicans would have acted against their own nature if they had not followed their own ways. *But* one of these ways is precisely — and this is decisive — a loving openness, a desire to learn from others and to exchange ideas with others, even when these others are at first unfamiliar and to some extent always remain unfamiliar. This rule of thumb is very important and useful for the discernment of spirits. Are the different churches in the world with their peculiar features willing to learn from one another? Or are they convinced that their own nature would be radically threatened and falsified if in an endless process they continue to assimilate more from others? We can safeguard and develop that which is our own only by having the courage to borrow from others.

The Church and theology should not go so far that, impelled by a love and tolerance that make no distinctions, they say Yes and Amen to everything. When a theologian seeks not merely to reflect on ancient dogma in ever new ways but squarely denies it, then the limit has been reached.

THE ROLE OF THE EUROPEANS

We take it for granted now that in the present era of a Church that has become a world-Church all missions either have already become autonomous churches, rooted in their own culture and supported by their own people, or that they are approaching this stage. That is why it is imperative that missionaries from Europe and North America have the courage to yield first place as soon as possible to native priests and bishops. I believe that even today these new churches are happy when Europeans and North Americans work with them — discreetly, as subordinates, but also actively and courageously. There are still many things that European Christianity can say to other cultures.

Of course, the opposite also is true. The Latin American Church can tell us quite a number of things about base Christian communities, and the Church of East Asia can share with us Eastern spirituality, which it has assimilated and made truly Christian. It will not be enough simply to exchange imports and leave them as they were in their country of origin. The present situation of a unified humankind demands that every people be a missionary for other people. We continue to have the right, and perhaps the duty, to send missionaries to foreign countries. But this is no longer a one-way street. What we need today is a real exchange, wherein each one gives and receives.

13

THE RELATION BETWEEN THEOLOGY AND POPULAR RELIGION

The purpose of this chapter is to present a few introductory, hence very general, considerations about the relation between popular religion and theology. We admit right away as our main point that, if scientific theology is to be true to its own nature, it will have to reflect on the religion of the people much more than it usually does. Yet this theme of our considerations is very obscure.

THEORY AND PRACTICE

We might, of course, try to answer the question of the relation between theology and popular religion by starting to explain the relation that exists between theory and practice. Whatever that relation may be, theology would be considered as theory and popular religion as practice, so that the general relation between theory and practice would be the same as the relation between theology and popular religion.

However, the conviction is gaining ground, for a number of different reasons, that practice is not simply the execution of an independently built theory, but that theory consists, at least in part, of a reflection on practice. We might conclude that theology, as theory and science, not only has a relation to practice, which it directs, but that it derives from practice, insofar as practice is the source, or at least *one* source, of scientific theology. This is true, even though this scientific reflection itself is a constitutive moment of practice, in our case of popular religion. However, this very general scientific foundation for a correct answer to our initial question will not be further examined here.

THEOLOGY AND POPULAR FAITH

It is not possible to determine the relation between theology and popular religion adequately without having a clear idea of them both. This, however, is extraordinarily difficult. Indeed, it is very difficult to explain what theology is. That makes it difficult as well to explain theology's relation to popular religion. A distinction is often made between theology and religious science, where theology is defined as the scientific investigation of the Christian faith, as this faith is taught in the Christian churches and as a given and normative value for theology. Such a definition of theology might be accepted, more or less, by Christian theologians who refuse simply to equate theology with a "neutral" science of religion. But by itself this definition cannot serve as a bridge between theology and popular religion. First, because this vaguely defined "theology" comprises quite different disciplines (systematic, historical, fundamental, dogmatic, theoretical, practical), none of which can be related in the same way to popular religion. Next, because this definition leaves open many questions that are of the greatest importance for the relation between theology and popular religion.

What faith (of the Church) does theology, in its own self-understanding, presuppose as its object of study? Only the one laid down in the canonical Scriptures? If the answer is yes, how may we then understand the relation between this kind of theology and popular religion? Would it be possible for theology to understand popular religion as nothing more than human (religious and sociological) objectifications falling under the judgment (of rejection or forgiveness) of Scripture? But if we accepted this understanding and were then to discover in normative Scripture itself ("sola Scriptura") more popular religion, and would thus again have to look for a canon within the canon, what then?

If we wish to emphasize more clearly and firmly the fundamental relation of theology to the faith of the *Church*, what Church do we mean? And how do we then explain the relation of theology to popular religion? Do we mean a Church that is organized hierarchically, with an apostolic succession, with a supreme magisterium? Suppose that, in our question, Church is meant clearly and exclusively as a magisterium with its institutional and juridical activities, would we then not have to understand the relation between the Church's theology and popular religion as simply the subordination of popular religion to the Church of the magisterium and its theology? Popular religion then would be lawful only if it put into practice the religion proclaimed by the magisterium and explained by its theology.

But if the Church, despite its institutional character and hierarchical organization, is the Church of the "People of God," a pilgrim Church, in which everyone not only receives but also gives and serves, is "popular religion" then not a constitutive moment of this Church of the one and entire people of God, whose faith is the point of reference for theology and the real object of its reflection? We would then still have to determine within this one Church as the People of God the precise relation, one to another, of the magisterium, official church doctrine, the life of faith, popular religion, and so on. But it would be impossible to deny that popular religion has a fundamental importance for theology (and not just the other way round). We will have to come back to this point.

RELIGION OF THE PEOPLE

Bridging the gap is very difficult, not only if we start from the idea of theology as a church science but also if we do so from the idea of popular religion, that is, the religion of the people. What do we mean here by "people"? Certainly not simply the "People of God" in its usual sense. If this were the intended meaning the statement "theology has an essential relation to popular religion" would be identical with the statement " theology has an essential relation to the faith of the Church." The latter statement could be rejected or doubted only by those who acknowledge, within the faith and the life of the one, entire Church, two essentially distinct realities: the genuine revelation of God coming from above, which we can clearly and safely separate from everything else, *and* the human response to it, conceived as something clearly distinct from revelation as such, from the pure Word of God. Therefore this human response might be called popular religion, even if it were practiced by the whole People of God, the sum total of all those who have been baptized and lead a Christian life. However, such a complete and clear distinction between revelation and the living faith that accepts it is actually impossible. That is why such an interpretation of Christian popular religion does not make much sense and is of little use.

The notion popular religion, the religion of the people, has meaning only if the term "people" is used as a sociological term. Then it would mean that not everybody necessarily belongs to this people, that there are considerable differences in ways of belonging to it, that therefore the religion of the people is not simply and necessarily the religion of all the members of the Church. The final and decisive point is this: Despite these qualifications, the religion of the people has a theological significance; its exerts on theology itself an influence that is to some extent normative and creative.

Let us examine whether these postulates for a popular religion may be realized, at least in their major dimensions. For the sociological meaning of the concept "people" there is no difficulty, even if such a "people" is presumed to exist in the Church. We might add that, for our theological reflection, the precise meaning of the term is relatively indifferent. It is up to the sociologist to find out whether this "people" is characterized by its lower level of education, by the idea of the "masses," by its economic standing, by its marginalization in society as a whole, by its inability clearly to objectify its thoughts and wishes in cultural creations, by its lack of social power, and so on. Such features are not necessarily mutually exclusive. It is ultimately a question of terminology, which feature is essential for the concept of people.

At any rate, there is such a "people" also in the Church, because these features belong to human beings and characterize them insofar as they are members of the Church, live in her, and are influenced in their religious life by these features. It is, for instance, evident that in the Church too there are differences in cultural levels and that these differences influence people's religious life. It is (another example) all too clear from history that differences in secular power held by individuals affect their position in the Church, although the gospels and the Letter of James warn against this.

So the only real purpose of our question is to know whether it is possible, and even necessary, for the "people" *in* the Church (as distinguished from the Church as the People of God), with their popular religion, to have a creative and normative influence upon (scientific) theology. It is clear that, if the answer is affirmative, we must also explain more precisely what this influence consists of. For in a revealed religion, one that admits an initiative of the God who transcends world and history, popular religion cannot by itself alone be the first and last source of theology.

REVELATION AND PEOPLE

It seems that we must answer the above question affirmatively. To show this I offer a few necessarily fragmentary remarks. First, revelation exists concretely only as a revelation that has been heard and is believed. Now, without having to accept the errors of modernism, we may say that the first addressee and recipient of this revelation that is believed is the human person in general. Because of God's universal salvific will and the need of a real faith in revelation for salvation, owing to God's universal standing invitation to accept divinization through grace, the human person is already the addressee of divine revelation. The prophets, on the other hand, the *legati divini*, those who announce revelation, are, to be sure, the authentic interpreters who put into words God's self-revelation which occurs always and everywhere through God's grace. But the prophets are not the very first and only recipients of revelation, sent to announce something that would simply not exist without this message. Humanity as a whole, under God's universal salvific will, is the first addressee of divine revelation. Yet this revelation has, and must have, its history, in which it must be expounded and become irreversible in the history of revelation. Humanity, as the first addressee of revelation, is naturally not just the sum total of individuals, but humanity as it always exists in social groups, in peoples, and in nations with their history.

The "people," this collectivity of which we are speaking here, always lives in the social groups that constitute humanity as the first recipient of revelation. It too is an element in the first addressee of revelation. Such a "people," in all its diversity, in whatever ways its religious life may be organized, is, for the most diverse reasons, not at all acquainted with those human pursuits that presuppose an intense reflection and attention, that is, with science and especially with theology. Now original revelation, as mentioned above, is addressed to the whole of humankind, because the possibility at least of salvation is given to all of humanity. And the "people" may be considered to be the recipient of original revelation that has been least influenced by theology as a product of human reflection. Theology, as a human undertaking, is subject to all the historical limitations of any human enterprise. On the other hand, the faith of the people, although exposed (as the history of religions shows) to countless deformations and corruptions, is, nevertheless, because it is not so freely directed by human beings, closer to that first source of genuine religiosity and real faith that consists in God's universal standing invitation to accept divinization. The superiority of popular religion to theology does not properly consist in the fact that the former has, through critical reflection, freed itself better from corruptions and misinterpretations of original revelation. It consists in the fact that popular religion is continually being unconsciously inspired and carried by original revelation, and it has not passed through the screen of systematic, hence narrowing, theology. That is why popular religion, borne by the power of grace, may spontaneously welcome and realize every human possibility, and, in that sense, have the courage simply to be human.

CHURCH AND PEOPLE

The "people" can and may exist in the Church as well, although as the community in which faith has become historically irreversible in Christ, the Church has the most developed theology. It is also the Church of the written word of Scripture and of formulated doctrine, which is already theology. But the Church would not be herself if she were not built and carried on by persons who are the recipients of God's gracious self-communication (as revelation and not merely as salvation). Every doctrine in the Church is ultimately an interpretation and a verbalization of this innermost divinization of persons in the Church, whether primarily as doctrine and proclamation or secondarily as theology. Proclamation and theology necessarily refer to this primitive revelation occurring as God's self-communication to the members of the Church. This self-communication that reveals God must be objectified here and now and translated into the human words of proclamation and consciously shared faith. It depends also on the previous self-awareness of the primitive revelation as guaranteed by God; hence it depends on the Church, along with the Scriptures and the magisterium. And this objectified faith of the Church in its turn depends on and refers to the primordial revelation given through the "unction of the Spirit," by which every individual is taught by God.

That is why the Second Vatican Council in its Constitution on the Church says that Christ fulfils this prophetic function not only by the hierarchy with its magisterium but also by the laity who possess a sense of the faith (no. 35). The same Constitution states:

> The body of the faithful as a whole, anointed as they are by the Holy One (cf. Jn. 2:20, 27), cannot err in matters of belief. Thanks to a supernatural sense of the faith which characterizes the People as a whole, it manifests this unerring quality when, "from the bishops down to the last member of the laity," it shows universal agreement in matters of faith and morals.
>
> For, by this sense of faith which is aroused and sustained by the Spirit of truth, God's People accepts not the word of men but the very Word of God (cf. 1 Th. 2:13). It clings without fail to the faith once delivered to the saints (cf. Jude 3), penetrates it more deeply by accurate insights, and applies it more thoroughly to life. (*Lumen Gentium*, 12, Abbott edition)

Of course, here this declaration of the Council refers to the whole People of God, which is the Church, and not merely to the people *in* the Church, of which we are speaking in this chapter. Yet what the Council says must also apply to the people in the Church, since they are part of the people that is identical with the Church. It would not make sense to deny to the people *in* the Church what we affirm of the Church as a whole. We can, of course, say of the people in the Church what the Council says of the *sensus fidelium* only insofar as this people is, and continues to be, part of the Church, living in intimate union with her other parts and her leaders. But when we attentively read the text of the Council quoted above it is clear that, although this *sensus fidelium* must remain in constant union with the magisterium, with Scripture, and so on, it does not simply proceed from them. For this sense of faith comes from the Spirit of Truth, the unction of the saints, and it is given to all.

POPULAR RELIGION IN THE CHURCH

This brings us to the point where we can start reflecting on the creative and normative significance of popular religion in the Church. God's revelation occurs as divine self-communication to the People of God, to the Church, and thus also to the people *in* the Church. It is heard only when this self-communication is perceived and accepted, not as theory, but more profoundly in the very living of human life, to which also belong — but not only — the spoken word and a beginning of reflection and theory. That is why revelation, when it has been heard and explained in theology, is a revelation that has already been mediated by the concrete life of its hearers.

This mediation also happens in the Church through the concrete life of the people in the Church. That is why, in a theology of popular faith, we would have to inquire how God's original revelation is also mediated by the religious life of the people in the Church and thus becomes a revelation that is heard and believed. We would have to inquire what is revealed in this way and only in this way. For we cannot suppose that every human reality (as life and as word) is equally fit to mediate every aspect of divine revelation. There exists a history not only of theology but also of faith and of the revelation contained in it. This history of faith and revelation is in part determined and kept alive by all that occurs in human history. That is why we must ask what contribution the people in the Church have made and continue to make to this history of faith and revelation through themselves, and through their life and history. It may happen that at times scientific theology does not notice this contribution, that it overlooks developments in the history of the people's faith and never catches up with these developments.

So the real and urgent question is: What does popular religion have to say to learned theology? It has something to say, not only because popular religion is the popular application of an official proclamation of the Church and of theology, but also because the people themselves (within the whole Church) are an addressee of primitive revelation.

14

SOUTH AMERICAN BASE COMMUNITIES IN A EUROPEAN CHURCH

T he purpose of this chapter is to present a few remarks about base communities. These remarks can only be very general and abstract; they cannot give concrete pastoral suggestions for the formation and success of base communities.

What is a base community? How does it compare with our traditional parishes? What can we learn from South America? Where are the boundaries between a sect and a prayer group?

WHAT IS PROPERLY MEANT BY BASE COMMUNITIES?

First, we might say: Every Christian community should be a base community. A base community cannot simply be understood as being in competition with or an alternative to a *real* parish. Wherever Christians come together and establish a Christian community, they must support each other, really love each other in a truly tangible way, help each other in need, and answer to each other. As Paul would put it, they must edify each other, that is, they must help one another to be genuine Christians who adore and love God, who look to Jesus Christ and his cross and resurrection, who, strengthened by this Jesus, assume responsibility for their own lives, and who love their neighbor as themselves, not only in word and theory but in deed and in truth. When Christians establish a Christian community of this kind, it is a base community. In fact, every parish should be a base community.

It has rightly been said that at present our communities are only groups of people who have a priest to take care of their religious needs. When this happens in a public gathering it is called a religious service. But in such a parish there is hardly any inner bond between people. That is why they do not constitute a base community.

Yet, during the last decades or centuries, we have seen in our countries remarkable substitutes for these base communities that should be identical with a true parish. In this country there have been Holy Name societies, sodalities, the Legion of Mary, the Catholic Youth Organization, and so on. In these groups there often was something that began to look like a base community. Members knew each other, kept together, looked together for ways and means of leading a common Christian life. They met socially, their religious and secular life coincided, at least to some extent. In short, these associations possessed something that should properly be realized in a parish: truly shared Christian life, in which everyone tries, as the Gospel demands, to help bear the burdens of others; where all, impelled by an inner feeling of solidarity, pray and work together and try together to solve the problems of life. The fact that formerly these active groups existed, as well as many others, shows that Christians of former times had not totally forgotten that a parish should not look like a place where a church attendant, called a priest, takes care, on an individual basis, of the people's religious needs.

This simple fact alone shows that there is a need for base communities. Christians are Christians insofar as they are brothers and sisters to one other in the Christian community. Otherwise something essential is lacking in their Christianity. Communities must become real at a certain place, in a common life. They should not be service stations where church officials try to satisfy the religious needs of individuals. Christians must come together to constitute their Church — always of course in communion with the hierarchy, always with their priests — through officially approved religious services and the reception of the sacraments. And even more importantly: By the very fact that they themselves constitute a Church, a local Church, they realize what is properly meant by a base community.

CONTACT AND UNITY WITH THE PARISHES

The need for base communities is obvious. Every parish should turn from being an administrative district in the care of the official Church into a real community of faith, hope, and love, into a pilgrim people. That is, of course, quite difficult in our countries. We cannot simply take over the organization and lifestyle of base communities as they exist in Latin America, where they have become the hope of the Church and of Christianity.

The expression "base community," which speaks today to the minds and hearts of Christians in our countries, is undoubtedly imported from Latin America. So we are naturally tempted to imitate the way in which those communities are organized there, especially in Brazil. In that country there are thousands of lively base communities that start from the grassroots, not in opposition to the official Church, but because Christians are aware that, wherever they really live in the faith and hope of Jesus Christ, they naturally come together in true community. Animated by that faith, they feel responsible for secular society and they naturally build base communities. That is especially true because of the shortage of priests in Latin-American countries; not every community can have its pastor, as was still customary thirty or forty years ago in our country, where even the smallest village had its own Church and its own pastor.

The example of Latin America, where base communities are numerous and active, may be a warning for us in Europe and in the U.S. and an incentive to build active base communities, especially since we are also experiencing a shortage of priests. But the way in which these base communities should be organized among us cannot simply be taken over from Latin America.

There are two reasons for this. We simply cannot overlook our many parishes and the way in which they are still set up among us. Almost nothing of the kind exists in Latin America; therefore base communities compete much less with traditional parishes, such as they are in our country. Of course, even in our countries there may exist small base communities that are not the same as a parish. When a pastor has no interest in religion and shows no initiative, it may happen, in certain circumstances, that Christians have the right, while remaining in communion with the sacramental Church, to come together to help each other, to read Holy Scripture, to pray together. They may do all this, even when their efforts are hardly aided and understood by this or that pastor who may be little more than a routine church employee. Nevertheless, among us a base community should, as much as possible, be organized in such a way that the parish itself becomes the base community of people who really live Christianity.

In other words, if base communities emerge among us, they have a more urgent responsibility to seek to make contact with and eventually to unite with existing parishes and pastors. We cannot act as if, here in Central Europe, we might use base communities to build up a Church that would ignore the rather bureaucratic Church of the traditional parishes and dioceses. That could lead to no other result than a number of small sects that would soon wither and die.

NO BLIND IMITATION OF SOUTH-AMERICAN COMMUNITIES

As mentioned above, in some circumstances, when Christians have no priest or do not find a priest with an active Christian faith, they may organize a small Christian cell, a base community. But in our countries such praiseworthy initiatives should not lead to sect-like small groups that stay apart from the clerical Church, from the legitimate administration of the sacraments and the authority of bishops. At least for the time being, this may not be a problem in other countries, such as in Latin America, but it would be a problem for us. Our base communities cannot simply be a copy of the South-American communities, because we have a legitimate and meaningful hierarchically organized Church that is still important and with which the base communities would have to compete. There is a *second* reason, of a more secular and social kind. In Latin-American society, where there are few secular organizations, a true Christian community necessarily has duties that it must fulfill and can legitimately fulfill, but which do *not* exist for our Christian communities. In our countries many social tasks, which must be fulfilled to make life more human, are assumed by secular society, so that these tasks are no longer the sole responsibilities of Christian community. When a woman is taken sick in a South-American rain forest and the nearest hospital is a hundred miles away, it is quite natural for her neighbor to nurse her and to take care of her children. In a society where people are hungry and perhaps even starving, and where the State does nothing about it, Christian charity sees that these people do not starve. But in a country with unemployment compensation, social security, and so on, many obligations have been taken over by secular society. They need no longer be fulfilled by base Christian communities.

During the Middle Ages almost all schools and hospitals were run by the Church. It would make no sense if the base communities, in order to be really Christian, tried to assume again these functions in education and public health, which secular society has taken over and can probably carry out better than a small base community. It may still make sense that a few really Christian schools are run by a religious order or a parish. But that adds nothing to the fact that today most schools are run by the State. Reviving medieval models along these lines, so that the Christian communities might have something to do, is a utopia, and not even a good utopia.

DIFFERENCE FROM A SECT

In our countries base communities are facing a difficult dilemma: Can they and should they — in order to be really active and useful — be more than merely religious organizations in the strict sense of the word? Or should they be communities whose only activities are praying, preaching the Gospel, and administering the sacraments, since they find no other fields of activity? Such is the dilemma that faces a base community in our countries. That dilemma should undoubtedly be solved in favor of base communities that do more than pray, worship, receive the sacraments, and preach the Gospel. It seems to me that a base community can be that only when, going beyond a pure abstract devotion, it becomes a group of people with a feeling of togetherness, a community, a real family, and a union of love. United in genuine Christian faith, this community should be a family where Christian love is not only preached but is actually practiced. Otherwise it would not be a base community, but would revert to the style of the parish, precisely the style we are trying to overcome by means of base communities.

Are there tasks and activities that go beyond the narrow circle of abstract and theoretical religiosity and that have not been taken over by secular society and its organizations? It seems to me that there are. Of course, a base community does not have to become self-sufficient for all personal needs, wishes, aspirations, and activities. Music does not necessarily belong only in a base community; we may attend concerts that have not been organized by it. There are countless aspects of adult education that do not have to come, as in a ghetto, from a base community. In such things a base community should clearly differ from a sect.

A sect is a religious organization that not only breaks away from the larger religious group for some reason but that also tries to provide everything for its members. They keep together for all human activities, they are afraid of the chilly winds of secular life, they are striving in fact for an ideal that, until quite recently, very strongly stamped the life of the Church and the faithful. My grandmother did not go to the public library or a secular bookstore when she wanted novels. She went to the library of the Borromeo Society. The books she gave us for Christmas also came through a gift certificate from the Borromeo Society. I have nothing against parish libraries. Why should they not exist, if they are well run and meet a true religious need, which today's secular libraries do not satisfy? But a modern base community should not try to realize the ideal of a sectarian community that is self-sufficient in all domains and for all activities. That would be wrong.

MORE THAN A PRAYER GROUP

What then are the human needs, not strictly religious yet truly human, that secular groups and associations do not fill and that might be tasks for a true base community? Of course, a genuine base community should be a community that prays together, reads and studies Holy Scripture together, and practices Christian charity. However, although we cannot simply imitate the South-American base communities, base communities in our countries too must be more than a group of Christians who, not satisfied with their everyday life, feel a religious need and look for religious activities. Much creative imagination is needed in order to discover and to realize among us today some of the possibilities for a base community. People everywhere complain that, despite social protection and organization, they feel lonely, they lack a warm trusting contact with others, and they do not feel that they can rely on others and love others. So there should be plenty of opportunities for a base community that does not wish to be just a prayer group in the strict sense of the word.

It does not follow that Christians should be able to find only in such base communities what they excel at providing. A more individualistic kind of Christianity is not excluded, where Christians attend Sunday Mass, receive the sacraments, read Holy Scripture privately, and keep up their interest in religious problems. Such Christians may live a good life and not belong to a base community. But there are certainly many people who feel alone, cold in their religious life, who experience a stronger desire to praise and adore God together with their brothers and sisters, who would like to speak heart to heart about religious questions and problems. There are certainly people who are convinced that they cannot practice real and unselfish love for others if they cannot, in a really Christian community, hence in a base community, meet others and help them bear their burdens.

There are certainly many people who rightly feel that they are far from having fulfilled their human and Christian duty of unselfish love, if they just pay their taxes to the State and contribute to the Red Cross and other praiseworthy organizations. Why then should there not exist real Christian base communities, in which people are united by the bond of love, that is by the Holy Spirit, and not only by human affection, where they not only praise God together but also help each other, whenever possible, to carry the burdens of life? Of course, no Christian should be obliged by any authority to belong to such communities. But there are undoubtedly many opportunities for them today, which we should discover with the eyes of love, and try to use in the power of the Spirit.

15

CHRISTIAN PESSIMISM

The following considerations have been inspired by what Paul says in 2 Corinthians 4:8. To describe, from the human point of view, his situation as an apostle, he dialectically uses the opposition *aporoumenoi all' ouk exaporoumenoi*. These words may be translated in many different ways: "sore pressed, but not destitute," "sometimes in doubt, but never in despair," "perplexed, but not even driven to despair," "at a loss, but never despairing," are a few translations in modern editions of the New Testament. They show how difficult it is to translate the Apostle's words.

Whatever the translation, this is the way in which Paul characterizes his situation as an apostle. He feels that this situation is a permanent, not merely a passing feature of his life. We may add, without demonstrating it further, that it is also a feature of Christian life always and everywhere.

The second part of this dialectical unity, as occurring in human life, *exaporoumenoi* (destitute, in despair) is especially obscure, because in the same letter (1:8) the Apostle seems to affirm of himself what he denies in 4:8. At any rate, it shows that the perplexity mentioned in the first part of 4:8 must be taken very seriously. We might say that, for Paul, Christians are people who live in radical perplexity. We might even wonder how we are able to see this existentiell[1] perplexity in every human dimension without abolish-

---

[1] The two spellings, "existentiell" here and "existential" later, follow the German usage. "'Existential,' as in Rahner's phrase 'supernatural existential,' refers to an element in [the human] ontological constitution precisely as human being, an element which is constitutive of [one's] existence as [human] prior to [one's] exercise

ing it, and at the same time how it is, in turn, enveloped and saved by what is specifically Christian. That is the question I intend to consider in what follows.

HUMANITY'S FUNDAMENTAL SITUATION

Our existence is one of radical perplexity. We have neither the right nor the possibility to ignore this situation or to believe that we can abolish it in any dimension of our experience. I need not point out, or bemoan in detail, the daily experiences that make us perplexed.

In the beginning of Scripture God tells us that we must rule over nature and her powers. When we do it we start misusing them. We invent all kinds of social systems, and every one of them turns without fail into an occasion of injustice and abuse of power. We claim that we are looking for peace among all peoples, and we get ready for war in order to find peace. The whole of human history is a perpetual swinging back and forth between individualism and collectivism, and humanity has never succeeded in discovering a permanent and universally acceptable compromise between these basic demands of human nature.

What matters here however is to understand that, for a Christian anthropology, this perplexity in human existence is not merely a transitory stage that, with patience and creative imagination, might eventually be removed from human existence. It is a permanent existential of humanity in history and, although it keeps assuming new forms, it can never be wholly overcome in history. This is an essential feature of a Christian pessimism. It does not matter here whether we explain this pessimism through the fact that we are creatures, and finite creatures at that, or through an appeal to original sin, or by making our ineradicable sinfulness an argument for pessimism.

Of course, we cannot say that human finitude and historicity alone explain the fact that history cannot follow its course without friction and without blind alleys. Nor can this Christian

of freedom. It is an aspect of concrete human nature precisely as human. 'Existentiell,' as in Rahner's phrase 'existentiell Christology,' refers to the free, personal and subjective appropriation and actualization of something which can also be spoken of in abstract theory of objective concepts without such a subjective and personal realization" (Karl Rahner, *Foundations of Christian Faith*, p. 16, translator's note).

pessimism be justified merely by the fact that it is impossible fully to harmonize all human knowledge with its many disparate sources, or to build a fully harmonious praxis on the basis of such disparate knowledge. We might also mention that we can never fully understand the meaning of suffering and death. Yet in spite of all this, the Christian interpretation of human existence says that, within history, it is never possible wholly and definitively to overcome the riddles of human existence and history, which we experience so clearly and so painfully. Such a hope is excluded by the Christian conviction that we arrive at God's definitive realm only by passing through death, which itself is the ultimate and all-embracing enigma of human existence. It is true that Christian hope has the right and the duty to project, in the empirical space of our human existence, an image and a promise of a definitive existence. But ultimately this is only the manner in which we practice faith in the consummation that God alone gives, that God's self is.

TASK OF CHRISTIAN PREACHING

People are afraid of this pessimism. They do not accept it. They repress it. That is why it is the first task of Christian preaching to speak up for it. We used to say that the Christian message must convince people of their sinfulness, which they refuse to acknowledge. Undoubtedly this continues to be a task of Christianity and of the Church. And today we may rightly emphasize it, because we are still to a great extent living in a period of euphoric belief in progress. That belief is still far from dead, although our recent experiences have led us to be more pessimistic about the human situation. But we take it for granted that better times lie ahead and that our precarious situation will be easy to correct. Preaching Christian pessimism is quite legitimate, because the Christian message is convinced that a great part of human suffering is caused by sin, so that, in the final analysis, to admit sin is the same as to admit suffering.

I wonder whether the Church is sufficiently opposed to the repression of Christian pessimism. We were quite upset when the Nazis reproached Christianity for speaking of a "valley of tears." Although I took part in the elaboration of *Gaudium et Spes* at the

Council, I would not deny that its undertone is too euphoric in its evaluation of humanity and the human condition. What it says may be true, but it produces the overall impression that it is enough to observe its norms, and everything will more or less turn out well.

It does not insist enough on the fact that all human endeavors, with all their sagacity and good will, often end up in blind alleys; that in questions of morality, when we really face the whole of reality, we get lost in obscurities which no moral formula can wholly remove. In short, as Scripture says, the world is in a bad way and it will stay that way, even if, as we are obliged to do, we fight against evil to the death. The Council wishes to get rid of triumphalism, but some of it has lingered on. The idea that, if only the unbelieving world were to accept the living Church and her message, it would find salvation and happiness, is subconsciously present and continues to be voiced frequently in declarations of the magisterium. That the Church herself is a Church of sinners, that even her true and salutary doctrines lead to riddles, that the Church too, in the final analysis, does not know exactly, clearly, and convincingly how we should go about it, is not the most clearly voiced conviction of the living Church.

TASKS FOR AN ACADEMY

Even Christians meet insoluble perplexities in every dimension of their existence. While the Church really has neither the power nor the desire to solve them, she must help people to admit their true situation or universal perplexity. She should be careful not to promote an unreal and un-Christian repression of this pessimism.

Might this not be the first, if not the last or only task, of a Catholic learned society? Such an academy is not supposed to be the source of cheap Cassandra-like prophecies, because this pessimism cannot be the pretext for a lame and cheap resignation. Its function is to explain situations in which we can act realistically, fight and win partial victories, and soberly and courageously accept partial defeats. But it really is a duty of such an academy to speak for a realistic pessimism, for an insight into our perplexed situation. Should it not tell all parties in society that none of them has a clear-cut formula for happiness, that all parties are lying when they act as if it were possible to discover such a formula, that political leaders act in a cowardly and un-Christian way when they are not ready honestly to admit the mistakes they have made? Should the academy not be a place where thought is honestly and soberly given to riddles in the Church's message, where the conscience of the Church of *sinners* may be voiced, where the praises of the Church are not sung in sacred euphoria? The Church's theology can no longer boast of that neo-scholastic homogeneity that has been customary since the time of Pius IX. Should it not be possible for such a fact to become evident at least in an academy? Should an academy not resist the current tendency to claim that there is unity in theology, where such a unity can honestly not exist? Such a claim is made only in order to place in opposition a militant, aggressive Church and a wicked world. Should an academy not be the place where human rights even in the Church are defended, because it is not evident that such rights are always respected in the Church? All unrest does not come from an evil source, every doubt is not destructive, not every fight is worse than a graveyard peace, not every little conflict is bad. The really bad situation would be if church leaders never had the courage to admit that, with all their good will and conscientiousness, they had made mistakes. Thus, for instance, I cannot help regretting that, with one possible exception, the mistakes of the magisterium under Pius X have never been officially rescinded. A Catholic academy should be a place that acknowledges the perplexities that occur in every dimension of human and ecclesial life.

It is obvious that this does not amount to a license for ceaseless grumbling in Church and society, or permission to fight the hierarchy in the Church and authorities in the State, and to reject their legitimate decisions. True pessimists, with all their perplexities, will be tolerant with regard to an existing situation, because they know that another, possibly preferable situation, for which they may certainly fight, will not be heaven on earth either. There is no need to glorify a pope in order to live with him in peace and obedience.

THE SOLUTION OF THE APOSTLE PAUL

What we have said above has not yet led us to the question brought up by the Apostle's two dialectically opposed expressions. For Paul not only tells us that, even as Christians, we will never grow out of our perplexities in this world, that we must see them and bear them, but also that in spite of them we are *ouk exaporoumenoi* (not driven to despair). It is true that as Christians we put our trust in God, and that we are freed and consoled in all our needs and fears by the Holy Spirit. It is for this reason that Christianity is a message of joy, courage, and unshakable confidence. All of this means that, as Christians, we have the sacred duty, for which we will be held accountable before God, to fight for this very history of ours joyfully, courageously, confidently. We also have the duty to bring about a foretaste of God's eternal reign through our solidarity, unselfishness, willingness to share, and love of peace.

Yet it seems to me that we have not yet mastered the problem of the two existentials put together by Paul. How can we be perplexed pessimists, how can we admit that we are lost in existence, how can we acknowledge that this situation is at present irremediable, yet in Paul's words "not be driven to despair"? Do these two attitudes not cancel each other out? Are there only two possibilities open to Christians? Do Christians simply capitulate before the insuperable darkness of existence and honestly admit that they are capitulating? Or do they simply ignore their perplexity and become right away persons who have victoriously overcome the hopelessness of life? Is it possible for Christians neither simply to despair nor overlook in a false optimism the bitter hopelessness of their existence? It seems to me that it is not easy to answer these questions theoretically. Yet the questions and their answers are of the greatest importance for Christian life, even if they occur only in the more or less unconscious praxis of life, and even if the very question about this Christian perplexity falls under the law of this same perplexity. This situation make it impossible to give clear answers to the questions.

The coexistence of these two existentials, which are not necessarily mutually exclusive, is evidently based on the fundamental difference between a knowledge that all persons can attain by their own powers and the knowledge that believers alone receive from God and God's grace. Because these two ways of knowing, and the truths known through each one of them, are incompatible, the two existentials may coexist in human life. Christians may feel the hopelessness of their existence, accept it without illusion, and for these very reasons be free, cheerful, and (in a certain sense) persons who have already arrived.

Christians, helped by God's grace, let themselves fall into the abyss of God's incomprehensibility and discover that this ultimate and permanent mystery of God's incomprehensibility is itself true fulfillment, freedom, and forgiving salvation. They experience their radical fall into the abyss of divinity as their deepest perplexity. They continue to experience this darkness, always more intensely and more bitterly, in a certain sense, until the dreadful absurdity of death. They see that this experience of darkness is confirmed by the fate of Jesus. At the same time, in a mysterious paradox, they feel that this very experience is sent to them by God and is the experience of the arrival of God near them. The perplexity and the fact that it is lifted by God's grace are not really two successive stages of human existence. God's grace does not totally remove the perplexity of existence. The lifting, the *ouk exaporoumenoi*, accepted and filled with grace, is the real truth of the perplexity itself.

For if it is true that we shall one day see God as he is, immediately, face to face, and if he is seen there precisely *as* the ineffable, unfathomable mystery that can be accepted and endured only in love, that is, in a total yielding up of self, then fulfillment for Christians is the height of human perplexity. Compared to it, all our riddles, our ignorance, our disappointments are but forerunners and first installments of the perplexity that consists in losing ourselves entirely through love in the mystery that is God. In the bliss of accepting the infinite mystery, that is, in absolute perplexity, all our partial perplexities, bewilderments, and disappointments disappear. The reverse is also true. As we expect and accept this end of our existence, our present perplexities are not removed, but encompassed. We are liberated, because they no longer dominate us. They have become the occasion and the mediation of our welcoming of the unfathomable mystery that gives itself to us and causes us to accept it in love.

While we are thus freed from every enslaving power and domination, the world remains what it is: the task, the challenge, the battlefield, with its victories and its defeats, as they succeed and overlap each other. We are unable to control them completely; we must accept them with their own perplexities. Within the ultimate freedom and even serenity of those for whom night and day, defeat and victory, are encompassed by the reality of God who is for us, nothing seems to have changed. We remain the *aporoumenoi.* And even the fact that we are more than saved and liberated *aporoumenoi* remains mysteriously hidden from us (often or forever, I do not know). But even then the fact remains that our perplexity is redeemed.

PART FOUR

Doctrine and Magisterium

16

WHAT THE CHURCH OFFICIALLY TEACHES AND WHAT THE PEOPLE ACTUALLY BELIEVE

If we consider the material content of the faith, nobody can deny that there exists a considerable difference between that which is explicitly and officially taught as part of the content of the faith and that which the average Christian in the Church knows about the faith and believes. Most Christians believe explicitly much less than what is explicitly present in the doctrine of the magisterium. This actual faith is to a considerable extent riddled with misunderstandings. Many things are held as belonging to this faith that in reality do not belong to it.

A PRELIMINARY REMARK

As matters stand it is not so easy to avoid the difficulty by insisting that, despite its weakness, the actual faith of these Christians includes the absolute assent of faith, whereby people believe, at least implicitly, all that the Church tells them to believe. For in their actual faith many Christians not only do not affirm this or that truth of the faith with absolute assent, they do not even affirm the absolute authority of the Church's magisterium (even in its definitive decisions) with an absolute assent of faith. Therefore it is not as easy as it might appear to avoid the difficulty by appealing to the implicit faith of the average believer.

True, the great majority of average Christians give an absolute assent of faith to this or that fundamental point of faith. Other points which may be true or false are held only in such a way that they do not destroy the absolute assent of faith that is also present in their mind. Their faith then really is a salutary faith. But this changes nothing in the description we gave of the average Christian, because the object of the absolute assent of faith, which for all that may indeed exist, is not precisely the teaching authority of the Church.

The difference between what the Church officially believes and what the average Christian actually believes has always existed. We might safely say that the pluralism of New Testament theologies is already a proof of it. One can distinguish, for instance, several levels in Origen's understanding of faith, and one is pressed to make theological heads or tails out of that. We hear of Christians who, as they were dying, professed their full assent to the faith of the Church. This implies that a material identity between the official faith of the Church and their own personal faith is not to be taken for granted and that eventually they wanted to make sure of that identity by this profession. Moral theology has inquired what truths of the faith have to be known and professed explicitly by all Christians. This question takes for granted therefore that there is a considerable difference between the official faith of the Church and the actual faith of many Christians. Attempts have been made, by the way, to narrow this difference by means of the doctrine that, in the long run, a positive atheism is not possible without serious subjective guilt. But it looks as if Vatican II has quietly dropped this doctrine.

So although the situation we are discussing has always been recognized to some extent, theological reflection has never probed it very intensively. Today it has assumed an important new aspect. Among average Christians of former times, those who could barely read or write (the "unlearned"), the awareness of the content of the faith might have been fragmentary and incomplete. But it was not opposed to other opinions, to other *Weltanschauungen*, because they did not exist in the consciousness of such people. A "primitive" awareness of the faith was, roughly speaking, matched only with ignorance. That is why in a feudal society, in which authorities decided on the faith of their subjects, one could suppose that everybody naturally shared the same faith and that there really existed Christian or Catholic peoples. This is no longer true today.

A fragmentary and imperfect faith coexists today with countless other ideas, many of which — at least as they are actually understood — stand in logical contradiction to the content of faith, whether people are clearly aware of it or not. It follows that the material defectiveness of actual faith is quite different from what it used to be. This explains why, as mentioned above, even the formal principle of faith, the formal authority of the Church, is threatened. Today's faith is not like the fragmentary faith through simple ignorance of former times, but coexists with positively contradictory elements in some kind of mostly unconscious schizoid state. Even if we suppose that no objective contradictions exist among the particulars in an individual's consciousness (statements of faith included), these contents are incredibly complex and almost impossible to harmonize. It is practically impossible for individuals to harmonize all the data of consciousness with the contents of the faith, although it is a tenet of that faith that such a harmonization is theoretically possible. This is one more reason why the gap between the official faith of the Church and the actual faith of the people differs essentially today from what it used to be.

THE REFUSAL TO ACKNOWLEDGE THIS

The first points to be mentioned about this fact is that it has not been sufficiently noticed by the official Church and that theology has not yet investigated it with sufficient care. Of course, as we said above, the fact is not denied and occasionally it is the object of some rather perfunctory theological reflection. Although we are aware of the fact, we relegate it to the edge of our consciousness. And in our official jargon, we continue to speak of "Christians" or "Catholics," wherever such people have not explicitly left a Christian Church or the Catholic Church or have not in some other way explicitly made known their total dissent from Christianity.

Thus "Catholics" are opposed to the new laws on abortion. Some "central committee" speaks in the name of "German Catholics." With the use of colors on maps, religious statisticians continue to designate regions that are more than 50 percent "Catholic." There is, of course, nothing wrong in this way of speaking, but the statistics have nothing to do with the inner faith of the people. They misrepresent the fact that the percentage of "practicing" Christians is quite low. Spain is a Catholic country, even though on Sundays only 10 percent of the people of Madrid attend Sunday mass. In theological discussions (for instance, with Hans Küng) official reports anxiously refrain from asking what percentage of Catholics might agree with the official position and what percentage might agree with the condemned opinion.

As a rule official announcements simply presuppose that those who read them have no doubts about the formal authority of the magisterium. That is why they generally do not take the trouble to explain to these "Catholics" the intrinsic reason for their decision. (A theologian who used to be influential in Rome told me once that this custom is quite legitimate, since it derives from the very nature of the magisterium. Defending the decision with rational arguments should be the task of theologians, not of the magisterium.)

This mentality takes for granted that Catholics are well informed. As a rule it does not try to address non-Catholics and the many very poorly educated Catholics. As a result, in their properly theological parts, important Roman documents of the Church use an esoteric theological language. They presuppose that their readers admit many things which these readers do not. They ignore fundamental theology and continue to use Scripture in the old way by quoting *dicta probantia*. In a word, the official Church and its magisterium presuppose, without ever saying so, that, when they address Catholics, they have to do with a relatively homogeneous group of people whose *Weltanschauung* contains, in fact, nothing but a clearly articulated Christian faith, together with a more or less absolute respect for the authority of the Church's magisterium.

While this situation, naturally, is not explicitly affirmed and many statements and actions presuppose the opposite, yet, roughly speaking, what we have said is true. In theory and practice, hardly any notice is taken of the extraordinarily large difference between the official faith of the Church and the actual faith of a large percentage of Catholics. This might open up to fundamental, dogmatic, and pastoral theology a wide field for reflection. I would like to add a couple of simple remarks, although I am afraid that they do not yet reach the heart of the matter.

POSITIVE THEOLOGICAL EVALUATION
OF THE DIFFERENCE

First, if seems to me that this difference does not have a merely negative value, but a theologically positive aspect as well. The fact that the *index systematicus* of *Denzinger* can rarely be found in the heads of ordinary Christians is not as deplorable as it may seem to many people who are tempted to identify saving faith with theological formation. Sophisticated knowledge of something may even be a great obstacle to its personal assimilation. I suspect that today's catechisms, however modern they claim to be, still contain too many things and that they do not present the heart of the Christian message, that which must by all means be said in a striking, really intelligible way. Moreover, it is the faith in the Church that actually exists in heads and hearts, and not properly official Church doctrine, that immediately and in itself is *the faith* that constitutes the Church.

Of course, we can rightly say that the often fragmentary and undifferentiated faith of the individual, and therefore also of many individuals, stands in relation to the faith of the whole Church. It is within the faith of the whole Church that the great and luminous totality of Christian faith is believed and practiced. One of its essential components is the faith of the saints, the heroes of faith, the mystics. But the Church does not consist only of its saints. The faith of the average Christian is not just a pitiable sketch of the official faith. It is a salutary faith borne by God's self-communication. It is really the faith that God's grace wishes to bring forth and keep alive in the Church.

We may not judge this faith by its objective verbal contents. Even when its objectification in words and concepts is very poor and deficient, it is still God's action in us, constituted by the self-communication of God in the Holy Spirit. As such, it infinitely transcends the most sublime theological objectification of the faith. The *depositum fidei* is not first and foremost a sum of statements formulated in human language. It is God's Spirit, irrevocably communicated to humankind, activating in persons the salutary faith that they really possess. Of course, the same Spirit also brings forth in this way the community of the faithful, in which the unity and fullness of Christian faith are objectified and brought to consciousness in what we perceive as the official faith of the institutional

Church. Nevertheless, what matters above all is the faith that really lives in the ordinary Christian. That is the faith that actually saves, in which God communicates himself to humanity, however pitiful and fragmentary its conceptualization may be.

Human transcendence, which is created by the Spirit of God, borne by God's self-communication, and enabled by God's self to aim at God's immediacy, is called faith. It always has a starting point in the world, a mediation, some individual "object" that is believed. But this mediation leading to ultimate salvation may, under God's Providence, be of different kinds. It may be paltry, it may be rich, and it has its own history. It is obviously not God's intention that every individual believer should enjoy all at once the fullness of this history of mediation — not even the faithful in the Church, although the Church makes possible a richer and more detailed knowledge of the totality of these historical mediations.

THE NORMATIVE SIGNIFICANCE OF POPULAR FAITH FOR THE MAGISTERIUM

These considerations allow us to say that the actual faith of the faithful in the Church has a normative significance for the official faith of the Church. The latter, of course, has a normative significance for the former, a point that is rightly emphasized by the teaching of the Church. Certainly we may not say that the faith of the magisterium should be directed by that of the faithful, as discovered by an opinion poll. That would be false, not only because of the very nature of the faith but also because it is impossible to discover, by the usual canvassing methods, what the faithful believe.

The official faith of the Church contains data that derive from the history of the Church's faith, data that have become irreversible and are normative for the faith of the present-day Church. The Church possesses an authoritative magisterium that is, in principle, normative for the faith of the individual, although this magisterium, while remaining essentially the same, is itself affected by historical change in its existence and its praxis. But this does not exclude the fact that the actual faith of Christians has a normative influence on the magisterium and on the official faith of the Church. However, this "normativeness" is essentially different from the one we attribute to the magisterium and its faith. These two influences *mutually* condition each other, although we must add that mutual does not mean equal.

First, it is obvious that, considered historically, the official faith of the Church depends for its growth and differentiation on the growth and differentiation of the actual faith of the faithful. Among them are theologians with their work, even though this work, just like the faith of others, in the Church, operates in constant dialogue with the Church's official doctrine. To put it with a bit of malice: *Before* the doctrine of the Council of Florence on the Trinity, theologians held a similar doctrine that had not yet received the blessing of the magisterium. The doctrine of the seven sacraments or of transubstantiation were theologumena *before* the Church's magisterium declared them defined propositions.

We should keep this in mind in looking at the last few centuries, when some popes have spoken as if the task of theologians consisted merely in defending and explaining the statements of the magisterium. If we do not want to make of theologians a special group in the Church, like that of the bishops, we must say that theologians belong to the People of God. To be sure, their concern is also the traditional faith that has already been officially approved. But it is broader than that. And whatever they work at, they do as members of the People of God with its concrete "theology." That is why their theologumena belong to the actual faith of the People of God, especially since they too may be called to order by the magisterium.

It is from these elements of the actual faith of the People of God that the Church's magisterium learns and should continue to learn. While it thus keeps learning, the magisterium declares that the doctrine discovered in this way is binding because it belongs to the actual faith of the Church and shares therefore in the infallibility of the believing Church. It follows that the actual faith of the Church has not only an actual but also a normative influence upon the Church's official faith. Distinguishing what merely happens to be present in the consciousness of the People of God from what is binding in faith may, in the final analysis, be a prerogative of the magisterium of the Church. The magisterium is then considered an indispensable component of the Church, as a community of faith. Yet it remains true that the faith of the People of God, as actually existing and not merely as officially approved, is a source of, and to some extent also a norm for, the official faith of the Church. Nor does it follow that there would have originally existed a believing Church without a magisterium (the first apostolic "witnesses") or that there would have been a time in which these two realities would not have mutually, although differently, influenced each other.

We might also put it as follows: In the eschatologically definitive and invincible community of faith that is the Church, there can be no teaching that would not be accepted by some obedient faith. That is why this obedient faith is also a necessary and rightful norm and criterion for the preaching of the faith, and not the other way around.

WHY THE ACCENT SHOULD SHIFT

The official faith of the Church is a norm for the actual faith of the Church. The faithful should be clearly aware of this. On the other hand, in its preaching, the magisterium should also pay attention to the actual faith of the faithful as it has always unconsciously done to some extent. It praised the devotion to the Sacred Heart after this devotion had already been promoted by the faithful in the Church. Countless such examples might be mentioned. However, in our age when people have become more aware of such things even in the Church, the question may be raised whether this influence on the magisterium by the actual faith of the people might not to some extent occur in a more conscious way, by means of surveys, adapted for this special purpose and different from other opinion polls.

This would not amount simply to a yielding to modern trends in the actual faith of the people. It might be possible that the official teaching from above is already being influenced by the faith from below, without noticing it, and that this would become clear only if this faith from below were better known. For instance, has the preaching of the possibility of eternal rejection of a person, that is, of hell, not become considerably more subdued during the last few decades, under the influence of today's general mentality? Whether this is a legitimate development is, of course, quite a different question and does not have to be decided here. It is not clear what form such "feedback" of actual faith upon the magisterium and its teaching should take. But it is certain that there can be no question in Catholic theology of withdrawing a defined doctrine because a considerable part of the faithful have refused to accept it.

However, this does not answer a further question: Should this widespread non-reception not induce the magisterium to give more thought to its doctrine (even if defined), to formulate it in a wider and newer context, and to remove the accretions that do not really belong to the faith and that may unconsciously adhere to a defined doctrine? Time and again, in the Church's awareness of the faith the accent has shifted. The history of dogma shows this very clearly. Would it not be possible today, prudently and discreetly, and with an eye on the actual faith of the people in the Church, to make such shifts consciously?

Let us take an example. The Church continues to give the impression that she makes known moral alternatives between which people must choose for their salvation or their perdition. That is the prevailing impression, while teachings about God's saving activity have a slighter impact. At the same time, compared with former times, people worry much less about their eternal salvation. Rather than feeling guilty in the presence of God they ask God to answer for the dreadful world he has created. Might not such remarks lead to a very important shift of emphasis in official teachings, without the need for the Church to deny any dogma that she has already proclaimed?

ACKNOWLEDGING POPULAR FAITH AND ITS CONSEQUENCES FOR CHURCH AND THEOLOGY

Even if we did not touch the real core of the question, it is easy to see that such considerations are important for ecumenical endeavors. Between the actual faith of devout Protestants and that of practicing Catholics (we are not speaking of their church organization or of their liturgy) there is today hardly any difference. In our ecumenical efforts should we not attach to this simple fact the importance it deserves? To be sure, in the eventuality of the unification of the Catholic Church with the Reformed churches, the Catholic Church would not withdraw the dogmas which the other side challenges. But does she necessarily have to insist that, when the churches have united, these dogmas be expressly taught by the magisterium as absolutely binding? This is really a valid question, when we see how the Catholic Church keeps very quiet about the fact that her own members do not accept quite a number of dogmas. It is a question when we see that the *filioque* does not have to be expressly mentioned everywhere in the profession of faith, when we may doubt that the procession of the Spirit "from the Son" and the procession "through the Son" mean absolutely the same thing. It is a question when we keep in mind the diversity of the material mediations of the one salvific faith in all stages of the history of salvation.

Our mentality today is not the same as it used to be. In earlier times people thought along simple either-or lines, or according to propositions to which an absolute assent was at least presumed. Today they rather presume that a simple either-or is a priori false. And propositions are as a rule affirmed conditionally, until, as is always possible, the opposite is demonstrated. It would be wrong to attach an absolute value to today's mentality. That would contradict its own nature. But even if we attach only a relative value to it, we may still wonder whether the differences between the Christian churches must be formulated in the same way in which they were and had to be formulated under a different mentality.

Can we seriously still think, as at the time of the Reformation, of an either-or with regard to the number of sacraments? If we take the modern mentality into account, might we not iron out differences concerning Vatican I, for instance, by explaining more clearly how the pope's decision is connected with the faith of the whole Church, by emphasizing more simply and clearly the fact that even a papal definition is historically conditioned, and so on? If the great regional churches in the Catholic Church have a certain autonomy, and if that also implies an autonomy of their theologies which do not simply echo Roman theology, something similar should also be true for the churches of the Reformation if they are again united with Rome. What this means more precisely should, of course, first be explained. And that would undoubtedly also involve some reflection on the actual faith of the people in the churches.

A last consequence of our reflections deserves to be explicitly mentioned. All salutary Christian faith must contain a moment of absolute assent. This assent, even as absolute with regard to the salvific and saving incomprehensibility of God, contains an empirical moment of mediation. But as pointed out above, this empirical moment of mediation has been incredibly varied in the course of salvation history. On the evidence of empirical facts, this moment in the Catholic Church has not always and everywhere been the infallible authority of the Church's magisterium. That authority is often questioned or ignored, and believers have in mind quite different mediations for their absolute assent to God's saving self-communication, for instance the Christ event or an unconditional hope.

That is why the Church's teaching should try to find the most efficient and obvious moment of such a mediation *in our time*. We should not preach indiscriminately everything that belongs to the fullness of the faith of the official Church. Judicious emphasis is needed. And it should be put where the actual faith, or a real possibility of faith, for humanity today exists. From this point of view too, the actual faith of people would have a (correctly understood) "normative" significance for the Church's official faith and teaching. This actual faith must certainly not be the whole of what is taught, but it should serve as a starting point. That may be a platitude, but it is a very important one, and one that is too often forgotten.

17

THEOLOGY AND
THE ROMAN MAGISTERIUM

Despite everything that has already been said in the traditional fundamental theologies and ecclesiologies, and despite many declarations of the Church's magisterium from the nineteen century until the second Vatican Council (and even recently by Pope John Paul II), the precise relation between the magisterium of the Roman Church and theologians remains very obscure. We need not expect it ever to be so lucidly set forth that conflicts between both parties would be excluded a priori, even if the rules were quite clear, easy to follow, and faithfully observed. Such an ideal and unruffled peace cannot be reached even with the best norms and principles. On both sides there are finite human beings, with a mutual incommensurability in thinking and willing that cannot be removed even by good will, Christian virtue, and the assistance of the Holy Spirit. Yet we might say that some principles could be stated more clearly than they have been, principles that would make for more peace and harmony.

The Roman magisterium takes for granted that for listeners of good will and with some theological formation its declarations are immediately understandable. This refers to the meaning of such a declaration as well as to the degree of obligation ascribed to it by the magisterium itself. It also takes for granted that in relation to theologians the magisterium has the final word, which theologians must simply respect in its (relative) binding power. More or less underlying such a declaration is the opinion that theologians' only

176

task is to defend these declarations of the magisterium (by showing how they derive from the primary sources of revelation) and to explain them, insofar as this may be required for a given cultural and social situation.

On the other hand, while readily granting the Holy Spirit's assistance to the Church, theologians remark that such declarations of the magisterium are also the work of theologians and that, as a result, they are affected by the historical and human limitations of their authors, limitations that are often quite evident. Such declarations must be examined by using a method that can be very complicated, because their unconscious presuppositions make them less clear than their authors believe them to be. Such an interpretation is unavoidable, although Roman theologians often dislike it. It gives rise to new formulations that are as correct as the previous ones, although they may not be too well received in Rome.

Theologians insist that it is not at all true that their work begins and ends with the declarations of the magisterium. In countless cases these declarations are the result of theological activity that from the start has not been directed from above. Theology can and must ask many questions that have not yet been settled by official declarations. Theology that has not been officially approved can be very important for the progress of Christian faith, in the world and for practical life. Theologians say that for this kind of work they need a certain amount of freedom and the opportunity to do research that is not controlled. They would be unable to do this kind of work if, from the start and at every moment, they were worried about avoiding the danger of erring, if uniformity in theology were desirable, and if a legitimate pluralism were suppressed as impossible or dangerous.

These demands of the magisterium and of theologians do not necessarily contradict each other. The trouble is that it is not easy to see how they can be easily reconciled. Also each "party" generally admits the demands of the other "party" sotto voce, while loudly defending its own side, as if in practice only that one really mattered.

We are trying to make some progress by attempting to formulate what each side must grant to the other more expressly than is usually done and try then to put it into practice.

SELF-UNDERSTANDING AND PRAXIS
OF THE MAGISTERIUM

Those who represent the magisterium should explicitly say in its name, and put in to practice, something along the following lines: We too are human beings when we make our decisions. We are men who should not be rash and full of prejudice, yet we cannot help being such. Abstracting from the fact that strictly binding decisions of the pope and a council are preserved from error by the Holy Spirit, we, the pope too, can err in our decisions, and we have often done so in the past. This is obvious and it does not imply that the magisterium is either illegitimate or unnecessary. It is our duty to work with this risk, because we have a duty and a function, even when the presuppositions and conditions of strictly binding decisions are not given, exactly as a physician can make diagnoses even when he is not absolutely certain of them. Moreover, you theologians do not have the right to assume that our decisions are wrong for the simple reason that they contradict the opinions that you, or quite a number of you, have defended.

On the other hand, we have a duty that up to now we have generally shirked. We should expressly indicate in a text that a given declaration is not absolutely binding. You theologians should understand that up to now we have not done this enough and thus have made it look as though whatever we say is absolutely binding, with no possibility of error. Of course, with our tacit consent, every ecclesiology says the opposite. But that is the only place where it is being said. It does not come to the knowledge, nor act upon the conscience, of the faithful. What the German Bishops' Conference said about this in its Königstein declaration of 1968 has unfortunately evoked little attention and imitation. In this way our official declarations too easily produce the impression that, for reasons of faith, not the slightest doubt may exist or be tolerated about their truth. That is where we should modify our praxis, not only saying that our declarations are really binding (although not all to the same degree) but also mentioning more precisely the degree and relativity of the obligation they impose. A few decades ago the magisterium ordered you expressly to indicate in your theology lectures the theological qualification of your theses. Why should we not do the same when we issue official declarations?

But you theologians must also help to bring about what is required for us to proceed differently in the future. If you or members of the faithful simply presuppose that a non-defining declaration has practically no importance, and so you lay it aside with a shrug and a smile, you must not be surprised if we speak as though our declarations were irreformable. So you must collaborate to bring about a spiritual climate in which authentic declarations, even when they are not strictly binding, really have some importance in the Church.

REACTIONS OF THE THEOLOGIANS TO MEASURES TAKEN BY THE MAGISTERIUM

There is a great variety of possible reactions. They have not been fairly described by the Council in *Lumen Gentium*, and they cannot be set forth exactly by means of general rules. When should a theologian expressly, head on as it were, come up against a declaration that is not irreformable? When and how might it be a theologian's duty to do the opposite (presumption favors this course) and expressly defend and supply evidence for a Roman declaration? Where might a *silentium obsequiosum*, an obedient silence, be desirable? Where and when would it be opportune to examine and evaluate a Roman declaration with due care, make the necessary distinctions, and in this way suggest corrections or possible interpretations not expressly seen in Rome? When or where would it be indicated to put the content of such a Roman declaration in a wider context which we have not explicitly thought of so far, removing from the start perspectives that are too short-sighted? In this way we who are also willing to learn may understand that, even if one ignores the immediate text of the declaration, that which we properly meant survives.

We are honestly ready to expect such distinctions and not to take offense at those who do not wholly agree with our provisional decisions. It may be desirable that a time of *silentium obsequiosum* not last too long before one expressly requests a revision. (The present pope speaks calmly of the Yahwist, whereas seventy years ago we would not have been indulgent toward a Catholic exegete who spoke that way.) For concrete cases, however, there are no general and easy rules to help us decide whether a reaction takes place for good reasons and with sufficient respect for the Church's magisterium. In such a judgment you may be wrong and we may be wrong. Especially since this is also a question of spiritual discernment. We cannot adopt as our policy that our reactions to your opinions must not allow the slightest possibility of a doubt or that we should not react at all. Everyone must expect that in such cases mistakes may be made and injustices committed.

While these points can be granted, no license is given to commit the sins of pride, rashness, or self-righteousness. Rather, we are warned to feel gravely responsible to fulfil our duty courageously, and at the same time to consider realistically the possibility that we may blunder. But you, as the Christians you want to be, must patiently bear the burden that is so often put on your shoulders without good reason or necessity. To be removed from office, to be condemned, is certainly not pretty, and you may defend yourself against it with every lawful means, and you may fight to insure that these lawful means are not withheld from you. But if all this does not help, then removal from office and other measures can also be the fate of a Christian, just as when some public authority or terminal disease puts an end to someone. Life is that way. In the world and in history things do not always work out smoothly when several people and groups fulfill their duties and avail themselves of their rights.

You should not a priori and in general deny the right of the pope or the bishops to take administrative measures as consequences of doctrinal decisions. When, for instance, a theology professor teaches candidates for the priesthood on behalf of the bishop, the bishop can and must eventually withdraw that commission if he reaches the conclusion that it is not being carried out in accordance with the faith of the Church, for which the pope and bishops are more authentic spokesmen than anyone else. Of course, we office bearers should proceed in all this with utmost prudence and fairness. Who among us would claim that this has always been the case? But there are decisions in the world that have to be upheld, even if one knows that they may offend against truth and justice.

STRICTLY BINDING DECISIONS

We come now to the cases where we are dealing with a strictly binding conciliar or papal decision. We office holders do not wish to demonstrate here and now, from the nature of the eschatological Church, that there must exist in the Church such strictly binding propositions of faith expressed in human words, and that we are not reduced to living in the truth without being able to grasp any part of it. We wish only to formulate a few practical maxims, some of them for us, some for you. If there are such definitions, it is evident at once that the magisterium cannot tolerate theologians who publicly, in direct confrontation, reject such truths of the divine and Catholic faith. Whatever may be the case with the private faith of individual Christians who absolutely reject for themselves certain dogmas of the Church, it is clear that no one may act as a church theologian and at the same time publicly reject church dogmas. Where that happens, the magisterium must intervene, officially declare this contradiction, and exercise the basic right to draw administrative consequences from this declaration.

But other cases are conceivable and concretely possible, in which theologians deny that their positions are irreconcilable with the Church's dogma, whereas the magisterium is convinced of the opposite. In such cases these theologians may, of course, be summoned to declare their express consent to the defined dogma and its normativity for their own theology.

When we go further and demand that they withdraw their own positions (*"laudabiliter se subiecit"*), of course, the situation becomes complicated, as we should admit more openly than we have done so far. In this case what does it mean to withdraw such positions? Does it mean that those theologians have reached the conclusion that their positions cannot be reconciled with dogma, although they had held the opposite opinion? How quickly do they have to reach this new conviction? How is it that we who speak for the magisterium have the right to demand such a declaration, since it is naturally also possible that we are mistaken when we assert that the positions are irreconcilable. After all, our assertion does not belong to the content of the revealed faith. Is the following attitude acceptable? A theologian has been censured. He or she claims to accept the dogma in question, and also the legitimacy of the way in which the Church formulates it. He or she accepts the imposed terminology (language used for a dogma that is not simply identical with its content) as normative for his or her own theology. As for the rest, the theologian holds on to his or her theological freedom of opinion, even if the Roman authorities do not like it very much in this case. Well, we in Rome have not yet given enough thought to such questions. And so we are tempted to treat you simply in the old-fashioned feudal way. We have not pondered enough what we want and what we do not want from you in questions of faith.

We in Rome cannot investigate the ideas of theologians with any precision. Their faith is based on a very complex process of consciousness, which is unavoidably an amalgam of correct propositions and a subjective way of understanding them. We cannot make sure whether, in all of this, that which must be believed in our dogma is really present, or whether it is practically eliminated by arbitrary interpretations and we are able to prove none of this. Moreover, in many other domains, the Church has already learned to distinguish in individuals a public and a private dimension and to avoid intruding into the private sphere. There are things that we ought to consider more carefully in Rome, so that we may draw conclusions from them with regard to what we may honestly and fairly require from censured theologians. In this respect we should find better formulas that no longer sound like submission formulas out of a feudal age. If, in this respect, a few fundamental adjustments were worked out, theologians would, in a concrete case, have to declare that they accept these general rules as applicable to their case. That would be enough.

It is not to be expected that in the foreseeable future pending disputes in theology will be decided through real definitions. We all agree that past definitions entail an undeniable obligation for your further theological work. It is evident that former definitions may not through your silence be driven into oblivion. On the other hand, we should admit that such definitions cannot be the beginning and end of your work, but that they can and must be "re-examined." Their meaning, the differences that exist between them and the interpretations that have been passed on with them without being identical with them, their meaning within the context of the whole of faith and of a new mentality, are not necessarily as clear and as unequivocal as today's preaching of the Gospel demands. It is certainly often the case that we in Rome, with its clerical milieu, do not notice how necessary such interpretations are, and that without them it is impossible, at least outside of Rome, to proclaim the Christian message in a convincing way.

REINTERPRETATION OF THE DOGMAS

It is quite possibly a sign of health and vitality that conflicts arise between the theology that we are traditionally used to here in Rome and the theology that you hold, as you interpret dogma. In these attempts and their evaluation by us both of us may have differences of opinion, we may get into conflicts and make mistakes. In that case (provided no theologian radically denies a dogma) everything that applies to declarations of the magisterium that are not strictly binding applies also to the interpretation of dogma, because the conflict is not between dogma and the denial of it, but between two interpretations, neither of which is infallible.

We should become more clearly aware in Rome that nowadays this work of interpretation is needed to a much greater extent than is actually being done or than suits our theological laziness. If basic dogmas of Christianity are to be announced in a credible way in a milieu that is not traditionally Christian, a reinterpretation of dogma is required that is much more extensive and intensive than your theology is already providing. What would an average Christian have in mind when he or she says that there are three persons in God? (I am afraid a heresy, which he or she considers to be a tenet of the faith!) If there is a history of dogma still going on, it is certain that the traditional formulas of classic Christology are not absolutely beyond improvement and that their meaning can be expressed in a different way.

In your thinking, theologians, you have certainly not caught up with all that an evolutionary conception of the world, a universal history of salvation, a positive significance for salvation of non-Christian religious, a positive interpretation of the divisions in Christianity, today's secular world, and many other things have added to your task. Moreover, there is also the problem of pluralism in theology, the problem of the different theologies of Africa, Latin America, and East Asia. Here are assignments that should render you humble and modest and inspire us only with good will toward you. We should rather be upset when you do not upset us, when dogma looks more like sacrosanct immobility than like living power.

Even a definition does not put an end to the history of truth. Our task in Rome is not merely to condemn. We must also make positive statements, that is, perform theological work in the strict sense. The pope cannot always write his encyclicals by himself. As a rule he should not. (Bellarmine cautioned the pope not to prepare his decisions by means of his private theology.) So we are in need of your collaboration. Why does the International Commission of Theologians lead such a pitiful existence beside the Congregation of the Faith, whose head has expressly refused to consult this international group of theologians? The theologians who belong to the Congregation of the Faith should have an international reputation, and it should be public knowledge which one of them has collaborated in a given decision. May we not hope that the Church would have that much openness?

ABOUT THE PROCEDURE OF
THE CONGREGATION OF THE FAITH

It stands to reason that, when the Congregation of the Faith has summoned a theologian, it must submit to him or her all the pertinent data of the trial in all its stages. It was still happening just a few years ago that a thick dossier was compiled against a theologian and printed up like a book, with numerous letters of denunciation, and yet it was forbidden to be shown to the theologian in question. Quite recently the *relator pro autore*, the counsel for the defense, who is officially appointed in such a procedure, was not made known to the defendant. He was not even allowed to know who would defend him. Such secretiveness is absurd and must end. In such things Roman authority violates human rights which the Church claims to defend.

I consider it also out-dated and impractical for the Congregation of the Faith to run the procedure in two different panels. A case is first discussed by the *consulta* of theologians. The result is then presented to ten cardinals, who alone make the decision. Of course, in the final analysis, the authority of the magisterium does not derive from the weight of theological arguments and the shrewdness of theologians, although the magisterium is obliged to use these means with the greatest energy. Yet this does not imply that the higher "panel" of cardinals alone should discuss and decide what will then be finally submitted to the formal authority of the pope, especially since these cardinals, *salva omni reverentia*, for the most part understand nothing of theology that is to be found outside their old textbooks. What harm would it do if theologians and a couple of really competent cardinals worked together from the start, even if the theologians were present only in an advisory capacity? One more remark: Such procedures should be terminated more rapidly. It is wrong for a theologian to have to wait in fear for many years until the Roman bureaucracy has reached a decision. Prudence and careful scrutiny do not justify such long delays. And in the international curia of a world-Church, which Rome claims to be, it should be possible for the colloquy between the theologian and the Roman authority to be held in all the usual international languages.

SELF-UNDERSTANDING AND PRAXIS OF THEOLOGY

On the other hand, theologians should say something like this: First, we are not a mafia, where everyone can speak in the name of theology and for all theologians. Neither do we feel obliged, whenever an individual theologian comes in conflict with Rome, to voice our indignation at once in the name of freedom and theology. Undoubtedly, we have the right and the duty to side with Rome against another theologian, when we are convinced that a Roman declaration is correct. Among theologians too cronyism is repugnant. Have we reached the point where theologians have compromised themselves when they support a Roman decision?

Collective declarations of theologians deserve the serious attention of the Roman authorities. In principle they should not ignore them. They should not think that every dialogue with theologians goes against the nature of the Roman magisterium, because according to canon law, it is "the highest chair" independent of any other human power.

Nevertheless such declarations are a questionable thing. The fact that they are frequently used in the world, that they are modern, is not yet a convincing argument for such collective declarations. They very quickly lose their usefulness. They easily indulge in generalities that nobody denies. God and the devil, however, are to be found in the details that such declarations often glibly ignore. Appeals for more freedom in theology are especially questionable and useless if they do not state clearly what they mean and what they do not mean.

ACKNOWLEDGING THE MAGISTERIUM

The first thing that we from our side, as theologians, have to say is therefore that we acknowledge our duty with regard to the Roman magisterium. As theologians we have, of course, an autonomous function and a pastoral responsibility in the Church; we are not just the handymen of the magisterium and church authorities. But the magisterium is for us theologians a binding authority, and we discharge our function within the hierarchical Roman Catholic Church and according to her rules. This task goes beyond a mere defense and interpretation of the magisterium, for the simple reason that the development of the faith in the Church cannot be adequately directed by the magisterium. At the same time, this task can be carried out only in basic agreement with the Church's magisterium.

As declarations about the relation between the magisterium and theology keep multiplying so quickly that nobody can keep up with them, we theologians should not in one breath formally acknowledge the magisterium, and in the next emphatically and emotionally demand our freedom. We should also insist somewhat more on how to respect the magisterium. The latter does not act presumptuously when it censures us. Such a procedure is not basically a threat to the freedom of our theological research. The relationship between faith and the teaching of it, on the one hand, and scientific theology, on the other, may be fluid and vague. Yet a theology that would have no connection with the preaching and the practice of faith would no longer be a Christian theology, but at the most a secular science of religion. That is also why there are no clearly delimited domains or methods in scientific theology that are absolutely outside the competence of the magisterium.

It has already been emphasized that there is a difference between publications of scientific theology and those intended for a wider public. Disregarding the fact that such a distinction is difficult to make, because the media inform everyone about everything, the distinction continues to make sense. It invites the magisterium to a greater tolerance toward scientific theological writings, especially when they are composed and written in the tentative and hypothetical way that belongs to scientific research. However, as long as theology does not degenerate into mere religious science, as long as it lives and thinks within the faith of the Church, scientific publications and periodicals cannot in principle reject the supervision of the magisterium.

On the other hand, we must now tell the Church's magisterium that we theologians do not clearly see, in many cases, what respect for the magisterium and the fact that it is a norm for us concretely requires of us and what it does not. That this norm has different levels and degrees follows from the official doctrine that all the declarations of the Church's magisterium do not impose the same degree of obligation. This situation entails a difference in our re-action to such declarations. But the magisterium does not at all clarify for us theologians what these differences are and what they are not. Or it publishes norms that are so vague that either they are false or they do not help us.

TO WHAT DO OFFICIAL DECLARATIONS OBLIGE?

If, for instance, the statements of *Lumen Gentium* (no. 25) about this question were absolutely valid, the world-wide dissent of Catholic moral theologians from the encyclical *Humanae Vitae* would be a massive and global offense against the authority of the magisterium. Yet the magisterium accepts this offense, showing that the norm of *Lumen Gentium*, and of many similar declarations of the last hundred years, does not describe precisely enough the relation between the magisterium and theologians. Should Catholic exegetes have kept silent so long about their problems under Pius X? They have respectfully done so and thus made it harder for educated Catholics to believe. What should moral theologians do with Roman declarations about sexual morality that they consider lacking in distinctions? Should they keep quiet, or should they contradict them and make the necessary distinctions?

The absence of more precise norms may derive from the difficulty of the problem. So in every case we ourselves have to look for a way out with courage and prudence. We cannot stop at being prudent, not even at the risk of our jobs; we must also have the courage to take risks, that is, we must consider the possibility of being censured by Rome.

But this does not quite answer the question. Suppose that the censure of a theologian or of a group of theologians is accepted by them with all due respect and docility, but that it is not certain that the traditional theology, the opinion that has to that point been held in the Church and to which Rome appeals, is identical with a clearly defined dogma. In such a case the formal authority of the magisterium is not irreformable. As history has shown, it has often been wrong. Let us further suppose that, despite an obvious docility, the arguments of the magisterium do not convince the theologian in question, and that we have to do with an important question, which implies that this theologian has a duty to speak for the truth, and which at the same time increases the interest of the magisterium. What happens in such a case? Is a *silentium obsequiosum* sufficient? Is the theologian allowed, is he or she obliged, publicly to contradict? If we say yes, what happens then to the "sincere assent" which the Council's decree expects from the theologian? If the disagreement is only on this one point, and the theologian maintains an inner respect and submission, how can the magisterium make sure of this? Should it be satisfied with this general attitude and quietly tolerate the disagreement on this point? If we say that, on this one point, the theologian should simply keep quiet, the important question arises how the progress of knowledge, which is necessary for the life of the Church and for the credibility of her teaching, can be assured since the magisterium may be wrong in such a declaration. If, for instance, all theologians had shown this "sincere assent" by an obedient silence with regard to the biblical decrees of Pius X, the present pope could not speak of the Yahwist, and no introduction to the New Testament would be allowed to say that Luke's Gospel was written after the fall of Jerusalem.

It seems to me that, after mature consideration, the theologian has the right, and frequently the duty, to contradict a declaration of the magisterium and to maintain his or her opposition. The magisterium could tolerate this contradiction and use it to improve its own arguments without suppressing the theologians that side with it. The best policy would be to let the question of which side is right be decided by ongoing discussion and by the future history of the faith.

TOLERANCE OF THE MAGISTERIUM
WITH REGARD TO THEOLOGY

The magisterium should not give up the right to put an end to a theological controversy by means of a decision. But this basic right does not mean that the magisterium should put an end to every discussion, nor that there are always good reasons for doing so, nor that a non-defining decision would always terminate a controversy in such a way as to preclude further discussion. Through its administrative measures, the magisterium can, in individual cases, unreasonably and unjustly curtail the freedom of theology. Such cases have happened and do happen time and again. Far be it from me to assume that every intervention of the magisterium is a restriction of the freedom of theologians. Yet I must say that the number of cases of unjustified curtailment of freedom that I have seen inflicted on other theologians during my lifetime is considerable. The situation is especially serious since the Holy Office is also responsible for measures that it requires superiors of religious orders to impose on their theologians.

Tolerance for statements of theologians who disagree with non-defining declarations of the magisterium has been widely practiced during the past few years. Is this de facto tolerance the result of circumstances, namely that, given the great number of cases, Rome can no longer "keep up" with them? Is it the consequence of a practical powerlessness that one would prefer to overcome? Or does it result from an insight into the legitimacy of such tolerance? We would like to think that the latter possibility is true, and we would be happy if Rome expressly told us so.

No end, not even a good and important end, justifies the means one uses to reach it. This principle holds for the magisterium, which must not yield to the temptation to use wrong means to attain mandatory and praiseworthy goals. It must respect the tolerance toward theological discussion that should be acknowledged by Rome. One of the questionable methods is the denial of the freedom required by theology, a denial that derives from a secret distrust of the power of truth. A dead orthodoxy is no true orthodoxy. Allowing a legitimate freedom to theology does not consist in making a few harmless theoretical declarations. It means that the authorities, while having the power of preventing it, allow a theologian to express an opinion that they consider false (although either side's opinion may be wrong).

Powerful people live in constant temptation. This principle holds even for the Roman magisterium, even if we presume that they act in good faith when they obstruct theological freedom. In concrete cases, theologians should not, as has frequently happened of late, react with proud and unkind moralistic reproaches, an attitude that does not quite reflect the spirit of Jesus. All human beings are sinners; all are tempted. Even church leaders are not presumed to be immune from these weaknesses in the exercise of their official duties.

That is why, with all due respect, we are allowed to call the attention of these leaders to the fact that the burden of proof does not generally rest with the freedom of theology, but with the curtailment of this freedom. Once more: Why does Rome itself not expressly state these evident truths? Is Rome afraid? Why does Rome not understand that such expressly acknowledged principles would not diminish, but rather increase, the authority of the magisterium?

18

THE PERENNIAL ACTUALITY
OF THE PAPACY

Presenting an ideal picture of a pope for the future should not mean that we criticize popes, past or present. The only certainty we have about the future is that it will differ from both the past and the present. If we do not wish simply to present a few dogmatic reflections on the permanent nature of the papacy, but to allow our thoughts to scan the future, we will have to give some thought, or at least indulge in vague conjectures, about what the papacy may look like in the near future.

Because I had already been invited once to relate my dream about the pope of the future,[1] I started to dream again. I dreamed about the letter which follows. Dreams, of course, are always quite arbitrary and vague. It is evident that they may tell more about the dreamer than about the thing dreamed. Even in dreams I cannot see the future. That is why what my pope writes remains necessarily very abstract, why it says nothing about the concrete future that an inscrutable Providence is also preparing for the papacy.

Vatican City
Rome

Dear Peppino:

Now your old friend has become pope. Which one of us would ever have thought this would happen when we were studying to-

---

[1]See Karl Rahner, "Dream of the Church," in *Concern for the Church: Theological Investigations 20*, trans. Edward Quinn (New York: Crossroad Publishing Company; London: Darton, Longman & Todd, 1981), pp. 133–42.

gether in Rome in the 1960s. You must have been startled when you heard the news. So was I. But we can do nothing about it and, to tell the truth, I am rather happy that an Italian has again become pope. True, the pope, as Peter, is bishop of the whole Church, but he is also bishop of Rome, in Italy. When we were studying ecclesiology, we never found out whether the pope is also bishop of Rome, or the bishop of Rome also pope. But he is bishop of Rome. And that might as well be evident in the person of the pope. I say this because, during the last few centuries, we Italians have not been any worse at discharging this function than have people of other nations. This is true even if the history of Italy during the last century has not been too glorious. (But don't worry, I will not speak much of Italy, except when speaking to Italians.) At any rate, this is the only cheerful thing in my election as pope.

Undoubtedly there have often been ambitious popes; you will admit that I am not one of them. When I look not only at the task but also at the situation in which I will have to carry out the papacy now and in the near future, I see no reason for being ambitious or for coveting such a job. There is no way to perform it as it should be performed; and in the years to come less than ever.

Peppino, during the coming months I will, of course, have no time for the luxury of writing letters. But I am thinking of Giovanni, our teacher, who said, "Don't take yourself too seriously." So get ready for a long letter from your old friend. By the way, for you I remain the old Leone, even if I am now called Paul VII, for reasons that I do not have to explain to you. Another reason for this letter is that it allows me to give some thought to how I myself view this pontificate. Before the election, as a cardinal, I never racked my brain about this. I let my colleagues do it. I am telling you what I think, because I expect your criticism. Peppino, for heaven's sake always be the kind of person who breaks through the haze with which people, and even cardinals, piously but stupidly surround the pope with their acclaim. It is quite possible — I am a normal man, who loves to be praised — that I will react crossly to your sober criticism. But this is your duty, as my friend and as a priest. And I will certainly not throw you out when you come to me. We may even have our meals together. Starting with John Paul II the court ceremonial became a little more human and reasonable. At the very start, as I think of my task, a few things come to mind that I want you to know. It is not a program for my administration. That will come out in my first encyclical, which I will soon have to write or ask someone to write for me.

First, I will be the kind of pope that quite a number of popes have been before me. I hope not to be the worst one (which is perhaps not so very difficult). I will live and act with the conviction, which we learned and made our own as Christians and young theologians, that my office possesses the fullness of power. Vatican I remains, of course, fully valid for me. Yet I must tell you now, vested as I am with this fullness of power, that this conviction, based on faith, has become quite mysterious to me. Do you remember, when we were students, how Congar criticized the titles given to the pope? I will try to see to it that, while maintaining the dogma, there is not too much talk of the "Vicar of Christ." Christ does not need a vicar; he stays with his Church, and even with her pope, in whose very weakness he remains effective. The practical demythologization of the pope has made much progress in recent years. There is no more tiara, no more *sedia gestatoria*. In a private audience a visitor no longer has to make the triple genuflection, thanks be to God! Certainly there are still plenty of antiquated customs in the Vatican that may have to go. That much I may be able to bring about. It is no easy task, because so many nice, pious people simply love this traditional ceremonial. Do you remember that, as a student, I said that I would like to see a pope playing tennis in white slacks? I will probably not go that far. And I know, of course, that even a mixture of Catholic dogma and an analysis of the modern mentality will not provide us with a concrete image of how a pope ought to live and rule. So I will certainly leave many things as they have developed historically, even though it is not evident that they belong to the nature of the papacy, as many traditionalists involuntarily and unconsciously feel they do. On the other hand, I would not like to be a pope who drags along too much old-fashioned baggage from the past.

THE BUREAUCRACY MIGHT BE SIMPLIFIED

For instance, I am not at all convinced that the enormous bureaucracy that has grown in Rome during the last two centuries follows naturally from the dogma of the pope's universal primacy. If, as we hope, the Holy Spirit not only helps the pope (although unfortunately, as we once learned, mostly through an *assistentia per se negativa*) but is at work everywhere in the Church, it cannot be necessary that every good, holy, and wise thing starting to grow in the Church should first be blessed by a Roman authority. What I mean is that the pope and his helpers should imitate God and operate with an *assistentia per se negativa*, that is, prevent what is wrong and not imagine that they are the only ones able to plant the seeds of new growth.

I intend to consider whether in the Roman Curia it would not be wise to employ only priests who have successfully performed normal priestly duties for fifteen years. That would eliminate some of the often-deplored arrogance and smugness that the Roman "staff officers" (read: the members of the curia) display in their dealings with the "frontline officers" (read: the bishops). Of course, I do not know yet what precisely can and should be changed in Rome. However, my Peppino's ideal of a pope, humble and poor like Jesus, will probably not induce me to leave the Vatican and settle in a simple house in Trastevere or in the Philippines, as Bühlmann had suggested when we were students. But the bureaucracy of the curia can certainly be simplified to a great extent, for the simple reason that a Church that is no longer the Church of Europe with a few outlying sections, but which has become a world-Church, can no longer be "ruled" in such a centralized way as before. I am the sort of person who likes to delegate responsibility and power, who does not want to know and to do everything myself. Exactly what this means, as I said before, still has to be settled.

It seems to me that a pope too has the right to be a normal human being, a struggling Christian, an individual among many others, and to show this without affectation, humbly, if you wish. At one time, both of us studied the history of the popes. Peppino, how many frightful, stupid, narrowminded, backward things have happened in that history! We say this even as we remember that this history is the inscrutable will of the eternal God and that not even the pope is God's private counselor. Of course, we will not repeat the horrors and stupidities of former times. But still should I not fear that, as pope, I may commit other stupidities, despite all my good will and honest endeavors? Human beings, and therefore popes as well, always perform their duties poorly. Otherwise we would not be poor sinners, finite creatures, who painfully grope along in history's darkness.

Even if I do not impute to any of my predecessors, or at least to my immediate predecessors, a lack of humility and modesty, it seems to me that today a pope may, even publicly, make this critical self-evaluation more clearly than it used to be done. Important people in the history of both the world and the Church used to have the idea that their legitimate authority would be jeopardized, if they let their "subjects" see that they too were only human beings who committed blunders. It is only after their death that church historians were allowed to discover faults, mistakes, or backwardness in a pope. But if I am convinced that even as pope I remain a human being who will commit faults, perhaps even serious ones, why would I not be allowed to admit this even during my lifetime? Is the mentality of people who really matter not such today that authority does not suffer damage, but rather profits, when its bearer openly admits the limitations of a poor and sinful human being, and is not afraid to acknowledge them? For the time being at least, I am willing to listen to public discussions in my presence, eventually to learn from others, and to admit that I have learned.

Even as pope I would like to continue to learn. Let people notice that a pope can err, make mistakes, be poorly informed, and choose the wrong kind of assistants. All of this is evident and I believe that no recent pope has seriously doubted it. But why must such evidence remain hidden and covered up? Peter allowed Paul to confront him to his face, and I suppose that Peter acknowledged that Paul was right. Even today a pope may allow himself something of the kind. I for one, lay claim to that right and I am willing, if necessary, to let my authority suffer a loss, which it would be my duty to accept.

A MODEST PONTIFICATE AS COUNTERBALANCE

Peppino, there is something else I want to tell you. I shall not be a great pope. I do not have the wherewithal. You know that too. We have never fooled ourselves; so much the better. So I will not have an inferiority complex if I look quite modest compared with the great popes of the twentieth century. To me that seems providential. I have a feeling that through their grandeur these popes had an influence in the Church that they probably never intended and that had its questionable side, an influence that I will try to offset with my more modest pontificate.

Is it not true? Have these great popes not involuntarily fostered a mentality in the Church that overestimates the pope's proper function, as it should be according to dogma, and as it was in most of the history of the popes? Does this mentality not imply that a pope must in all respects be the greatest one in the Church, a point of reference for all initiatives, a teacher who is superior to all thinkers and theologians, a saint and a prophet, a man who conquers all hearts with his fascinating personality, a great leader who molds his century and makes statesmen and other great personalities pale into insignificance, a pontiff, whom all bishops respectfully approach, like petty officials before their king, in order to listen obediently to his words and orders? Peppino, I will not become such a pope and I do not consider it necessary at all. The pope has a task in the Church that is strictly limited, despite the universal jurisdiction and the fullness of teaching authority mentioned by the First Vatican council. I will exercise this fullness of power, but within the limits imposed on me by the limitations of my own nature. That, and nothing more. I will not be the holiest one in the Church. Before God I am less than the saints who live today in the Church, those who pray in silence, those who are mystically enraptured, those who perish for their faith in the prisons of the enemies of Christ and the Church, those who love unselfishly, as Teresa of Calcutta did, all the unknown and unrewarded heroes of everyday duty and abnegation. Nobody can deny that even an Innocent III pales before Francis of Assisi, and that the popes named Pius of the last two centuries are less important than a Curé d'Ars or a St. Thérèse of Lisieux. You may say, of course, that I am comparing realities that cannot be compared. However, in the life of the Church and before God's eternal tribunal, saints and great theologians, like a Thomas Aquinas or a John Henry Newman, are more important than most popes, and especially more important than I will ever be.

There are many charisms in the Church, and the pope does not have all of them himself. If it is true that we can really understand only our own charisms, even a pope must tell himself that he cannot evaluate everything that develops in the Church, and that God alone, and not the pope, stands where all that is good and holy in the Church merges into a perfect symphony.

That is why no harm will be done if my pontificate corrects, to some extent, the mentality of those pious Christians who wrongly expect from the popes what they can receive only from saints and great minds in the Church and possibly from themselves. Are there Christians, and perhaps popes, who remember that when they pray the Our Father with impatient hope for the coming of God's eternal kingdom they are praying also for the end of the papacy? An insignificant pope too may be providential.

However, I confess that I feel responsible for real progress in ecumenism, and I fear God's judgment if I were not to do absolutely everything in my power to promote it. During the past century all sides have been asserting that the churches have no right simply to go on as they have since the separation of East and West and the Reformation. We can say that, during the last fifty years and especially since the Second Vatican Council, a great deal has happened in the ecumenical domain. I am quite willing to admit that some people have done excellent work. But we may also say that we have not made real progress. The great churches are still disunited, and the rapprochement that has been growing between them does not change that fact. I wonder desperately whether this must go on.

Of course, the unity to which all Christians are obliged does not depend only on Rome. But I wonder whether we might not do more, even though we have been convinced up to now that we have done everything possible. I do not know how to proceed from here; I really do not see it. But I will honestly say that I do not see it, and I will ask others where they see new possibilities of making progress. I am determined to have the courage of ecumenical probabilism. In other words, I feel obliged in this question to try all measures and steps that are proposed to me, where no clear veto of my faith or conscience speaks against such measures and steps. In this question we must push to the utmost limit of what is theologically possible, we must adopt the tutiorism of boldness. Why, for instance, should we ask more for unity in faith than we, in fact, require today from people within the Roman Catholic Church? Why should the Christian churches, with their long histories, not be allowed to go on existing as partner churches and particular rites within the one Church? Why should I not be allowed to declare expressly that neither I nor future popes will proclaim an *ex cathe-*

dra decision except when we are in clear and obvious agreement with the body of bishops of the whole Church, to which the other churches too will belong as permanent partner churches?

Did Pius IX and Pius XI not act in this way when proclaiming such decisions? Why could we not expressly consider such a procedure a valid norm? Would it not be possible to assure the leaders of the churches of the Reformation, expressly and solemnly, that in the one Church these churches will enjoy at least as much autonomy and historical continuity as Rome grants to the partner churches of the East? It simply has to be possible to make progress in the ecumenical question. If I admit that all persons are of good will, have honest motives, and are open to the Holy Spirit, I can simply not believe that, as some would say, "for the time being, unfortunately, nothing can be done."

INTELLIGENT EXPERTS INSTEAD OF
SOLEMN DIGNITARIES

During the first years of my pontificate, I will advance very slowly, intentionally so, because I am convinced that it is impossible to devise a program for the Church's history and life in the crucible of abstract theology and without the help of secular futurology. In the era into which we are clearly entering the Church will have to do more ecclesial futurology and programming of her future than she has done up to now. I will not convoke an ecumenical council, and it is for me still an open question whether the synods of bishops in Rome are the best way to achieve what I have in mind. I would prefer to call together a group of intelligent theologians, sociologists, futurologists, and historians. Such a group would exhibit real competence, courage, and a certain amount of creative imagination, and would try to formulate how the Church should proceed, insofar as it is possible to plan such things. We have to develop a strategic pastoral plan for the world-Church. Nothing of the kind exists as yet.

Today in the secular world, in society at large, history is not constructed step by step in some improvised way. Rather, history is planned ahead of time. Well, the Church too should do something of the kind. Especially now that she has become a world-Church and is no longer the self-confident Western Church, exporting missionaries all over the world with the help of European colonialism.

As yet I do not see clearly what I have in mind. Today, humankind is clearly interdependent in all its parts, economies, and cultures, such as has never existed before. In order not to perish, humankind has had to come to a self-awareness that was impossible in earlier times. Thus it actively assumes, in a wholly new way, the conscious responsibility of its own future. The world-Church faces a similar new situation. My new group of experts in pastoral strategy should tell me and the Roman congregations exactly what this new situation is.

The canon law of the universal Church cannot remain in the twenty-first century what it was in the 1980s. In a world of enlightened rationality, of technical civilization, of a global interdependence of all cultural powers, the preaching of the one and forever valid Gospel message cannot proceed as it did in the beginning of the twentieth century. Then we had the Church's antimodernism, her reactionary distrust of all profound social and economic change. We must change our methods, and we must do it consciously and intentionally. We must ask ourselves in a new and explicit way how the Church's responsibility for peace and justice is to be carried out in ways and forms that we do not even suspect, that perhaps we even oppose. Liturgy throughout the world must not forever be the Roman liturgy translated into the vernacular. Is the valid hierarchical structure of the Church wholly reconciled with all the social changes that have been introduced, or at least planned, and that also have a right to exist in the Church of the future?

Undoubtedly the Christian message will remain what it has always been: that God gives himself in grace and in life eternal, that this and nothing else is the end of all evolution, and that it has been definitively and irrevocably promised to us in Jesus, who died on the cross and rose from the dead.

But this message must also be expressed in wholly other ways; it must be seen from wholly other points of view and in wholly other contexts than those we learned long ago at the Gregorian University in Rome. And the old message may grow in itself, not only in the way we express it. What else would really be the meaning of the Gospel's word that the Holy Spirit will slowly introduce us into all truth? This "progress" cannot be brought about by the pope or by the Congregation of the Faith. What we can do here in Rome is to encourage others to work for it and to respect courageous efforts, even though they are not always the final word in wisdom or orthodoxy. Despite all the pluralism in theology that cannot be abolished today, it is still possible to see where the true substance of Christianity is being impaired by foolish or brash theologians and then have the courage to stop them. For theologians are not the highest court in the Church.

I would like to write an encyclical showing that we can express the fundamental truths of Jesus' message in a way that differs from the one we are used to because we learned it in school. Will I ever be able to do it? I doubt it, because such an encyclical will not speak of relatively secondary points in the "hierarchy of truths," which is rather easy to do. I will have to say, against every form of atheism, that the living God exists (and we ought to understand atheism if we wish to overcome it), that God has come among us in this world and in this history (although the reality that is distinct from God is billions of years old), and that the experience of death is not the ultimate experience.

Of course, one who teaches what is highest and most important may be somewhat behind the times with regard to what is less important (otherwise the eternal kingdom of truth and love would already be here). But that must not mean that the Church (as in the centuries since the Enlightenment) should always be afflicted with a certain old-fashioned clerical futility. I am afraid that there are people in Rome (and naturally elsewhere as well) who try to justify this stance with profound ideological reasons such as "the folly of the cross," or "Christianity can never be fashionable," and try to push Rome's activity in that direction. That was also Lefebvre's idea some time ago.

THREE FACTS MUST BE KEPT IN MIND

My good and faithful Peppino, I want to tell you something. I hope that during my pontificate I will not forget three things (in addition to many others naturally). *First,* for two million years, human beings had to seek and were able to find the eternal God without a papacy. That is a truism, for the papacy is conceivable only at "the end of time" after Jesus Christ. But that truism deserves to be kept in mind especially by a pope. Strictly speaking, the old ways of finding God have not been abolished by the papacy. They have only been strengthened and radicalized. Theologians should give more thought to the question of how a headhunter in the Stone Age, who pierced the head of the foe he had killed, might have anything to do with God, with eternal life — and this in Jesus Christ, without passing him by. Theologians should not take the easy way out by referring to the Second Vatican Council, which on this question speaks of "ways known only to God." Ultimately I too am saved in ways known only to God, yet I must try to understand them. And people today can accept that only in Jesus Christ will they find their salvation, if they can understand, to some extent, how this possibility also existed for those who lived before Christ.

The *second* thing I would like not to forget is that there are still today countless persons for whom the papacy does not exist, and whose consciences are often challenged in life and death-threatening ways: The billions of Chinese, the people who live in societies where atheism is the state religion, the hundreds of millions of Muslims, the millions of baptized Christians who acknowledge Jesus Christ as their Lord and Messiah and yet do not want to have anything to do with the pope, the other people whom we usually call "pagans," the many Catholics who, in fact if not expressly, feel nothing for the papacy. Yet even in this final phase of salvation history, in which there is a papacy, I have a right and a duty to hope, and even in my way of acting to presume, that all these people find the God of Jesus Christ, in whom everything moves and has its being, and reach God as their eternal destiny.

If this is true, the papacy, although objectively binding, is not the highest or most fundamental truth in the hierarchy of truths. It is a reality and a truth that can be reached by inference only by those who have already found God in Jesus Christ. It is also possible that countless persons who find God and Jesus Christ are unable to make this inference, without any fault of their own. They may even be convinced that the papacy cannot be inferred from their basic faith or that they are forbidden to make such an inference. How modest, how prudent, how mild a pope should be before this world, for which the papacy is either unknown or, at most, a strange happening in history.

A *third* point must influence my way of acting as a pope in the world. The pope has to be a witness to the basic truth of salvation that concerns all human beings. But, as he preaches the Gospel, he must not give the impression of believing that he can solve all the problems people meet in their private or public lives. I cannot tell any man what woman he should marry, although for him this is an important matter for time and eternity. During our studies in the sixties, we both noticed how many questions of capital importance the sociology of the Church could not clearly answer, but had to leave to secular intelligence and to history's experiments. Although these issues are of great interest to many people, there are thousands and thousands of questions in the human and natural sciences for which the Church has no answer. I do not have the slightest doubt that the Christian message about God and eternal life in Jesus Christ, when properly conveyed and really accepted, has a strong and creative importance for our life on earth, for both individuals and society, with regard to the problems that ultimately they have to solve by themselves. But that adds nothing to the fact that, like everyone else, a pope, when his message about eternity concerns concrete human problems, must entrust the world to God, to God's inscrutable grace and the historical freedom of human beings. The pope has no prescriptions that must be followed as exactly as possible so that nothing but peace and happiness may reign in the world.

Despite its great importance for the Church and the world, the papacy is only one factor in the strife and harmony of a world that God alone grasps and directs. These things are evident, of course, and it is to be hoped that no pope has ever doubted them. But I will do my utmost never, in my conduct or in my words, to produce the slightest impression that I have forgotten these obvious truths. I will speak gently and modestly. When presenting to people the truths of the Gospel that are so important for their everyday lives, I will always, in a true dialogue, ask them how these truths can be translated into the reality of their lives, something that I cannot clearly know from the start.

THE CHRISTIAN MESSAGE AND SECULAR KNOWLEDGE COMPLETE EACH OTHER

The truth of Christianity is not subject to the secular self-understanding of human beings or of their sciences. Yet, if we really wish to understand this Christian truth, we need an ongoing dialogue between those who announce the Christian message and those who voice the secular self-understanding. God has not willed that this double knowledge fully exist in a unified way in a single human being, not even in a pope. Undoubtedly the pope must lay claim to the teaching authority that Christ and the Church have given him; he must speak like one who has power and not like the scribes; but he must always also convey his message in open dialogue.

I will try to speak and to be silent in such a way that my words and my silence may reach the immense multitude of those who cannot yet acknowledge the papacy as a reality of their faith. I will speak and be silent, aware that the true message can reach its fulness only through dialogue, when it has been accepted by human self-understanding in a synthesis that ultimately God alone, and not the pope, brings about. I believe that this is the real reason why the full doctrinal authority of the pope must shun any kind of triumphalism.

Peppino, with all these reservations, I believe in the papacy and I accept it as my task, according to the teaching of the holy Catholic faith. What then is the true nature of the papacy, as it operates in word and sacrament for the whole Church? We live in the endtimes, even if that end lasts a very long time. Who knows how long it will last, since human beings now have the power of committing collective suicide? "The end of times has already come and the renewal of the world has already and irrevocably begun" — words of the Second Vatican Council that theologians do not ponder sufficiently.

The true and happy outcome of world history is irrevocable. It consists in the communication of the absolute God to his creatures. By dying on the cross and rising from the dead Jesus has made it irrevocable. That is the reason for the papacy; to this it is the basic and definitive witness, from this it derives its task and its fulness of power. Because this message can never die, because this message is one that can never be surpassed, this message about the end of time is also the promise that the gates of death will not prevail against the papacy during this endtime until the Lord comes, who will also put an end to the papacy.

The message and the messenger will always be with us. That is why it is ultimately a secondary question how many people acknowledge as legitimate the messenger who, at all events, brings a message announcing the salvation even of those who believe that they are not allowed to acknowledge the messenger! That is why, to my mind, the question of the visible success or failure of the papacy during my pontificate should not bother me too much. My pontificate will not be very glorious. I do not have what it takes, and God is not obliged always and in every instance to make up for the shortcomings of those who convey his eternal message hesitantly and inadequately, but truly.

Peppino, I believe that what the fourteenth chapter of Matthew says about Peter is as important for the papacy and for me as the scripture texts that are usually quoted. I am a Peter who tries to reach the Lord by walking on water, who always fears that he will drown, whom Jesus time and again takes by the hand and brings into the boat that really reaches the shores of eternity.

Dear Peppino, I wish to bring up something else, even if I cannot finish my letter today. If that is impossible, I'll go on tomorrow. Listen: My head is as empty as it used to be when we faced our examiners at the Gregorian. I must admit that I really do not know more about what a pope is now than I knew then, when we studied the doctrine of the papacy in ecclesiology. Of course, I also know what I have learned from experience during the past few decades, although this experience itself is for me a problem that I find difficult to solve. I am discovering in myself what the Second Vatican Council says about the pope, that he receives no new revelations. Although this is very much the case with me, I hope for God's help. But because this help is very unobtrusive it is very difficult to distinguish it from human considerations and impulses. So, I do not know more about the papacy than you do. But I know that the doctrine of the papacy, like all other truths of our faith, is surrounded by all the obscurities that, despite the greatest possible conceptual precision, lead into the mystery of God. I know that the doctrine of the papacy is valid throughout all time, like all the other truths of our faith, although we express them with concepts and images that are somehow — in different ways, of course — historically conditioned. I know that all these statements about our faith, including those on the papacy, stand in history and are therefore mixed with "accretions" (as we used to call them) which do not belong to what has been revealed. These accretions are recognized as such only in the course of time and are then removed. Then, the truth that is meant and asserted is stated once more under other historically conditioned concepts and images, but we are not yet aware that they too are conditioned.

Do you remember how years ago we used to speculate about transubstantiation, as defined by Trent, and how we wondered, without doubting what was meant, what we might mean today by substance, since we do not even know whether atoms and sub-atomic particles can be considered individual substances in the way in which the Fathers of Trent conceived of the substance of bread and wine. I do not have to insist on this or to bring up examples of other dogmas in which it is clear how an eternal truth of the faith is stated with concepts and images whose problematic and questionable nature is noticed only much later. You know enough examples of this kind, and even then we said that it is impossible to avoid the difficulty as easily as Pius XII thought, by claiming that in such dogmatic statements we have to do with concepts whose meaning and validity are evident to every mind at all times.

And now, Peppino, I suddenly wonder, much more intensively than I used to, what consequences the above-mentioned evident facts have when we apply them to the doctrine of the papacy and the pope's universal primacy of jurisdiction. That primacy exists; I am convinced of it. But what exactly does it mean? The Church's doctrine speaks of a *plena potestas*. But what does that mean and what does it not mean? I believe that there never was a pope who did not know that his power had limits. That is clear. The pope cannot create an eighth sacrament. He cannot make the Letters of Ignatius part of the canon or remove an epistle from the canon that some people consider "insipid." I cannot command you, Peppino, to become a Carthusian, or tell them to admit an old fellow like you. The pope's fullness of power is undoubtedly limited. True, I do not doubt that eventually I would have the competence of the competence (I do not have to explain to you what this is). But if this full primacy of jurisdiction has its limits, imposed by both divine and human law, and, what is more, if the pope may be forbidden, for *moral* reasons, to do something which we cannot prove lies outside his *juridical* competence, where then are the precise limits of this full primacy of jurisdiction? It would, for instance, be impossible for me to impose upon the Eastern Uniate churches the procedure for appointing bishops that has become customary in the Latin Church. It would be impossible for me to prescribe Latin as the language for the Eastern Church, somewhat as Muslims have made Arabic the language for the recitation of the Quran all over the world. I cannot at my whim impose upon a religious order, which grows through the free decisions of its members, every conceivable (maybe even reasonable) rule of life, which these members never envisaged when they joined it. I cannot transform the Jesuit order — whether I like it or not — into an order of discalced priests.

All these things are evident. As a rule they are respected in church history for the simple reason that the opposite would simply be impossible to carry out. But this does not mean that, in concrete instances, a pope does not, in good faith, transgress the limits of his fulness of power.

That is why I would like to hear more precisely from canonists where these limits are, not only in general but also in particular. Such limits exist, as I said, in the governing as well as in the teaching authority of the pope, limits that may in fact be transgressed. Was the Church allowed and obliged to give up all claims to the Papal States only under Pius XI? Did the wise Leo XIII not assign to Thomas Aquinas, whom both of us love so much, a position and a function in Catholic theology that an individual theologian simply cannot have? Have we not, by appealing to papal primacy, tried to force on the Eastern Church norms that, speaking plainly and honestly, belong among such transgressions? You can probably think of other instances. I intend not to commit such transgressions. I intend to see clearly, insofar as this is possible, where the limits are that I may not transgress. And that is why I would like professors of dogma and canonists to examine this question more accurately than they have done up to now. I will not cut them short at once if they do so loudly and become guilty of infringing their own limits.

Something else worries me on this topic, even if I may tell myself (thanks be to God) that during my pontificate, which will be very short, these difficulties will not become much more serious than they are now. The concepts describing the duties of a pope in governing the Church derive from our own culture and history. That is why we may suspect that, unknown to us, they are mixed with certain accretions that do not really belong to the revealed truth itself, although we are unable to separate them from it. It is obvious that such a fact has practical consequences. What happens when doctrine (with the praxis made lawful by it) has to be transferred, "inculturated," into other cultures? Such cultures exist, of course, and they have equal rights in the Church as a *world*-Church. But their way of thinking, of feeling, and of living is quite different from ours in the West. Although the West long ago ceased to dominate the world, it has not readily given up the dominance it still enjoyed in the Church during the nineteenth and twentieth centuries. I often think of this problem, although it cannot be solved during my pontificate.

There are other questions too that worry me and that I cannot evade during my pontificate. What I have written to you undoubtedly shows that I must be very prudent, very tactful, when I have to use my authority in doctrine and government. Such prudence and discretion do not mean, of course, that I might not act or make decisions. I must have the courage to act, even if my action entails the risk of initiating developments whose final outcome cannot be foreseen or of eventually slowing down developments that will gain acceptance in the future. That belongs to the burden of history which even a pope cannot shake off. Does it surprise you then when I tell you that, for all these reasons, I wonder already whether or not I should remain pope until I die. I am allowed to resign, if I realize that this would be more useful to the Church and if I am willing to do so. But might it not happen that I live to an age when I am no longer able to understand this, and when, in spite of my senility, nobody can depose me? A frightening thought! Or maybe, in the final analysis, a comforting thought, because it shows that, even in the Church, God's gracious Providence does not accomplish everything through the activity of a wise and strong pope. We will see.

It is time to stop. I have come to the end of my sheet and of my time. And yet I have not told you most of what I wanted to write to you, my old friend. What I have written is very imperfect and problematic. And I would not like (I am joking) to submit this letter to the Holy Office. Burn it when you have read it. Drop in soon. Friuli is not that far from Rome. *Patet porta et cor magis.* I hug you.

Your old friend Leone, who is now called Paul VII.

P.S. Our old friend Rosa recently died. Both of us have become the poorer for it.

19

UNDERSTANDING
THE PRIESTLY OFFICE

M any years ago I published a short essay on preliminary questions concerning an ecumenical understanding of the priestly office.[1] I do not have the impression that my paper has attracted much attention. I suspect that Protestant ecumenists feel that in this essay I stated the obvious, as I painstakingly tried to make plausible something that for them is absolutely evident. I suspect that there are some Catholic ecumenists who agree at least with the basic thrust of my paper. They share my conviction that the opinion, traditional among Catholics, of the invalidity of orders in the Protestant churches (at least, as a rule) and of what this implies for the validity of the Lord's Supper and the words of absolution is not above all doubt. But generally speaking, and especially in the statements of the official Church, my work has been courteously ignored. Moreover, they speak as if the ancient denial of the sacramental validity of orders outside of the Catholic and Orthodox churches would, in the future too, remain a point that brooked no discussion. I cannot, in the pages that follow, tackle this problem again as a whole in all its details. So this is an outline of the considerations that belong to this group of questions.

---

[1]See "Pseudo-Problems in Ecumenical Discussion," in *Theological Investigations 18*, trans. Edward Quinn (New York: Crossroad; London: Darton, Longman & Todd, 1983), pp. 35–53.

THE SACRAMENTS AS SIGNIFYING AND AS EFFECTIVE

Our traditional Catholic position on the ecumenical problem of the priestly office derives almost naturally and tacitly from a conception of the activity of the sacraments that I consider too narrow and that, nevertheless, implies consequences for the problem of the priestly office.

Our conception of sacramental powers (the power of celebrating the Eucharist, of confirming, of forgiving sins in the sacrament of reconciliation, of anointing the sick, and of ordaining priests) presupposes (if we use a traditional scholastic term) a rather narrow efficient causality of the sacraments. This conception forgets the well-known axiom that the sacraments are efficient causes of grace *insofar as* and because they signify this grace. If the priest who performs the sacraments brings about the sacramental grace in the way in which we usually think of efficient causality, it is evident that he does not, by himself, possess the power of exerting such a causality. He must receive it from elsewhere.

Now the way in which such a power is passed on is a very special one, without which the imparting of such a grace and other sacramental operations (transubstantiation and so on) are simply not possible. According to this conception of sacramentality, the fact that sacraments are signs has no decisive influence on our way of understanding their effectiveness, that is, sacramental causality. It is merely an additional statement that is added to the statement that they are efficient causes of grace. Strictly speaking, in the traditional doctrine of the sacraments, we should say: *Sacramenta significant gratiam et efficiunt* (the sacraments signify grace and bring it about), but not: *Sacramenta significando efficiunt gratiam* (the sacraments bring about grace by signifying it). Only the second proposition would state the deepest understanding of the Catholic doctrine of the sacraments. That understanding is contained in it, yet the usual totally objectifying explanations tend to obscure it.

If we want to see what might follow from this for the question of priestly office, we must show just *what* the sacraments "signify," that is, ritually make manifest in space and time within the Church's social dimension. It would be erroneous and would dim the nature of the Christian eschatological expectation of salvation, if we were to think that the sacraments simply and in isolation signify only the grace that is here and now imparted to the individual recipient of the sacraments. If this were so, the sacraments would signify only that which they still have to produce. But prior to this and beyond this they are the manifestation, in space and time, of the grace that has its origin in Christ, which has irrevocably and victoriously been introduced into the world.

Because of this eschatological irrevocability, this grace presents itself, through its becoming-manifest concretely *ex opere operato*, to individuals and to their freedom, and is (normally) accepted by them. Of their very nature the sacraments are the becoming-manifest of God's grace in Christ, which has become eschatologically irrevocable.

If we were to substantiate this statement in more detail, we would have to describe the very special nature of the possibilities of salvation originating from Christ. We would have to describe the nature of the Church as eschatological sign, the *sacramentum salutis mundi* (the sacrament of the world's salvation). We would have to explain that only through the eschatologically sacramental nature of the Church can we really explain (without using magic) the true meaning of the fact that the sacraments work *ex opere operato*. Today we know from biblical theology and the history of dogma that the sacraments cannot, with historical plausibility, simply be traced back to words by which Christ would have instituted them. Yet, in all truth, they must derive from him. So we would have to show that the real sacramentality of the sacraments and their provenance from Christ can be rendered intelligible only if they are conceived as basic activities of the Church that derive from Christ and is the real fundamental sacrament of the world's salvation. This fundamental sacrament is the permanent historical tangibility of God's self-promise to the world in Christ. The sacraments are the innermost activities of the Church, in which she actualizes her own nature in individuals. We would have to show that this is the only way of settling the tiresome old dispute about the number of sacraments.

The reality of the Church, as an indissoluble unity of truth and grace, on the one hand, and of historical tangibility, on the other, underlies the activities of the sacraments. It confers upon them their nature and their effectiveness. It is this ecclesial reality that the sacraments originally "signify": *significant ecclesiam ut sacramentum salutis mundi* (they signify the Church as the sacrament of the world's salvation). What the sacraments signify first and foremost is not what they bring forth, but that which brings them forth and which they are enabled to signify because they are brought forth by it, that is, by the Church.

HOW THE CHURCH BECOMES MANIFEST
AS BASIC SACRAMENT

If we may presuppose what has been mentioned briefly, that sacramental operations refer to the historically and socially tangible manifestation of grace and salvation that bestows on them their reality and power, the question comes up precisely *how* we are to conceive of this disclosure in space and time of the *sacramentum mundi*. The question comes up whether such signifying disclosures of the manifestation of the one *sacramentum mundi* at a certain place and time may not be considered to have many degrees. They might be called sacraments only under certain presuppositions. We may not deny that other activities in which the sacrament of the world becomes manifest also have a positive Christian significance and power. Some of these activities are: praying together in the name of Jesus and the religious rites that we Catholics call sacramentals. Actually, sacramentals exist under other names, with other theological interpretations, everywhere in the Christian churches. There are undoubtedly, over and above the signs of salvation offered by the Church that we call "sacraments," other signs that, for whatever reason, are not and should not be called "sacraments," although they are genuine attestations of the fundamental sacrament of salvation called Church, and they share therefore the effectiveness of that fundamental sacrament and its properly sacramental testimony.

Such social-historical and ritual references to the fundamental sacrament that is the Church, whence they derive their meaning and power, may be classified in quite different ways. For instance, they could be classified according to their content, according to their user, and so on. Such references should be considered legitimate. They constitute the historical becoming-manifest of the fundamental sacrament when their content refers to it in the right way, when they appeal to it, and when they are performed with Christian faith. More cannot be required for the legitimacy of such references.

What makes these signs into legitimate references is not that they constitute that to which they refer. It is rather the fact that what they refer to already exists: the Church as *sacramentum salutis mundi* and God's salvific will, by which God has already offered himself to every human being. Moreover, we must presume, unless the opposite is proven, that those who use this sign have the right disposition. This presumption is sufficient for the validity of such a reference, since, where the Church uses signs that are undoubtedly valid, such a presumption about the presence of an "intention" is presupposed and considered sufficient. In this connection it is also clear that the legitimacy of such a reference does not require a priori that these signs be used expressly within the juridical sphere of the Roman Catholic Church. If this were so, the Church would be unable to admit the validity of baptisms conferred by heretics.

Of course, it might be objected that for every sacrament, except baptism, the very nature of the sacrament may suppose conditions for its validity that are not present when the one who performs the rite has not received Roman Catholic ordination.

However, even then this ritual action refers to the objective and permanent fundamental *sacramentum salutis mundi*. It is performed in Christian faith, with a holy intention, in a church, in a religious environment, in which the good faith of those who perform it must be taken for granted. Where then would be the distinction between a sacrament that is valid for traditional Catholic theology and such a rite outside the normal Catholic sacramental order? It seems that it would consist in this: In the first case, we have to do with a "normal" sacramental signifying action. In the second case, we have to do with a sign that stands outside this normal order, with the result that it cannot be called a valid sacrament. This supposes, of course, that we have adopted a terminology that calls such a sign a "sacrament" only when it is used in the "normal" Catholic sacramental order. But is this the only possible terminology? And even if we say that it is, must we then claim that a ritual referring to the universal sacrament of salvation, a ritual performed in faith outside the "normal" order, has no effectiveness? Would the normal sacramental order in such a case not stand above God, although God is above this order and cannot be subject to it, when the fact that it is not observed implies no fault in those who perform the action, and when in a concrete situation it is impossible to observe the "normal" order?

There exist certain important subjective events inspired by grace (for instance, the implicit "baptism of desire") among persons who have never had any contact with explicit Christianity. These events cannot be called "sacraments," although they bring about or deepen justification. But does this certainly and clearly show that we must call every ritual action invalid if it is performed by somebody who is not, according to Catholic norms, validly ordained (although according to these norms ordination is normally required for validity). All sacramental signs, including the usual ones, hold their efficacy from a previous, ever present, eschatological salvific situation called Church. And this situation is witnessed to (in ritual words) even where this is not done and cannot be done in the usual way that the Roman Catholic Church imposes. Is the Roman Catholic Church's right to impose norms for the validity of the sacramental signs so apodictic that it excludes even the possibility of exceptions?

These are questions for which I wanted to suggest a few viewpoints. There are only questions, without any clear answer. Our whole discussion presupposed, without mentioning it, something that Protestant theologians do not admit, namely, that the question of the validity of orders is asked here from a Catholic point of view, that the Catholic administration of the sacraments is therefore presupposed as the norm. It is with this presupposition in mind that we have asked whether the non-Catholic administration of the sacraments (the Lord's Supper and so on) may be considered valid even when it does not comply with the usual Catholic norms for celebrating the sacraments. Naturally, Protestant theologians will immediately reject this presupposition of our considerations. They will refuse to confront the ritual ceremonies of their Church with the question of their validity according to the Roman norms. Yet even such theologians might be interested in the question whether even the Catholic doctrine of sacraments might not eventually admit (even for cases other than baptism) the validity of Protestant orders and their exercise in a more comprehensive way than is usually the case in traditional Catholic theology and preaching.

20

BOOK OF GOD—
BOOK OF HUMAN BEINGS

I n our innermost being there exists an uncanny awareness of our
creaturely finitude, whether or not we admit this awareness or
whether it has reached the surface of our consciousness. And
just as in nature where the groundwater is fed by rain coming from
above, so the hidden ground-knowledge of our creatureliness is fed
ever anew by the experiences of humanity in its history and through
its sciences. To this basic knowledge belong the mysterious experience we all have of being afloat in a world that is billions of light
years old, and the experience therefore of the frightening relativity
and insignificance of all that individuals, as well as humankind in
its totality, do and experience in their concrete life situations, in
the short history allotted to them within the enormous timespan
of the universe.

HUMANKIND IN THE UNIVERSE

When we think of ourselves in relation to the universe, we seem
like puny ants hauling a small pine needle a few inches at a time
and considering this an important achievement without realizing
how insignificant their laborious efforts are on the earth as a whole,
which is itself only a tiny mote of a universe that extends over billions of light years and continues to expand in an enormous burst
of energy. Viewed from this creaturely experience of our unim-
portance, whatever we do or undergo, whatever we consider as

214

happiness or fear as misfortune, all vanish into insignificance. Considered from a cosmic point of view, the most horrible thing that we might fear for all of humankind would be like a bit of friction in the enormous machinery of the universe. This might lead us to think that the whole history of humanity is basically nothing but a small, forlorn anthill in a universe that, among countless other things, has brought forth, incidentally as it were and quite indifferently, this three million years of human history to let it, after a brief time, wither away and die.

Yet the reality of the universe is in fact totally different from what this experience of our nothingness and forlornness in a cosmos ruthlessly going its way tries to make us believe. First, because this enormous power and energy that posits the cosmos in its reality and keeps unfolding it into an endlessly growing diversity is the most simple, most radical unity. This unity does not itself expand with the cosmos and thus disintegrate with it into multiplicity, but as one and as a whole, it is everywhere totally present at every point of the cosmos. This primordial power, which as an undivided totality subsists omnipotently everywhere at ever point, we call *God*.

However, this God, who in his entirety and omnipotence is present everywhere — even in the fir needle that the tiny ant is dragging along — has, in his power and overflowing love, freely decided to communicate himself, to insinuate himself entirely into this universe at a few seemingly forlorn points in it. Indeed, God has let this whole universe, in its apparently immeasurable and enormous size, come into being only so that the stage might be set for the occurrence of that divine self-communication to what is not divine, a self-communication that does not divide or scatter God, but bestows him entirely on the universe.

The points at which the universe is not only borne by God's undergirding power, but at which God is received in his unity and totality, are called human persons. To make possible this inconceivable marvel of divine, self-lavishing love, human beings must have already received from God an infinite openness and receptivity for God. The clearest sign of the fact that such an unlimited openness and receptivity constitutes human nature consists in the fact that human beings can objectively represent themselves to themselves, as well as all parts of their cosmic environment and the universe as a whole. It consists in the fact that in the tiny part of the universe inhabited by humans the whole universe finds a place, that in their consciousness human persons are always at once parts of the universe and parts that know about the whole — they are "ants" in which the whole universe is enacted. Persons with this infinite capacity can and should accept and experience God in his infinity, incomprehensibility, and freedom; they should accept and experience God as such and possess him as the absolute future beyond which extend no more possibilities.

Are there still other places in the cosmos in which, individually, the cosmos as a whole is aware of itself and which also receive God's own infinity? We do not know. But we might in connection with our question think, parenthetically, of the angels. We do not have to think of them as realities that exist absolutely and from the start beyond a material cosmos. If we admit that they too have a relationship, albeit a more comprehensive one, to the material cosmos, then our question, whether on other planets there also exist personal spiritual beings who receive God's grace, would already have been anticipated. Or, at least, it would lose a special actuality and importance. Really, the cosmos, which at first sight frightens us so badly, crushing us into insignificance, helps us to realize the importance, the uniqueness, and the definitiveness of humankind and of human history, as Christian anthropology has always held.

MEETING OF GOD AND WORLD

We must now make clear that the event in which through humankind the cosmos is aware of itself and its origin itself has a history. This history is an ultimate ongoing unity in a multiplicity of single events, in which humanity gradually reaches self-awareness and the free self-communication of God. Ultimately, the whole cultural and religious history of humanity is identical with this history, in which humanity increasingly becomes aware of itself and of the fact that it is called to God's immediacy. This is not the place to discover more precisely how the enduring fundamental structure of this history stands in relation to the real changes and significant breaks that occur in it.

It may be quite difficult to make out whether and how this history of humanity is the history of an ascent and a progress toward higher perfection in the most diverse dimensions of being human. But Christian faith is convinced that, in the history of humankind, there have been decisive breaks and periods that subdivide this whole history and direct it toward something definitive. If there were not, Christianity would not speak of the Old and the New Testament, of a covenant of God with Israel, of the new and eternal covenant of God with humanity in Christ.

From this basic perspective of the history of the cosmos and of humankind we Christians may say: The new and definitive stage of the history of the cosmos and of humanity consists in this, that at least in humanity (although maybe elsewhere too) the world has come to itself and to the conviction that its real end is its immediacy to its ultimate origin. And this is so, not only as a possibility presented to human freedom but also as a reality already existing for the future through the victorious power of God. In other words, although the history of the cosmos is always a history of freedom, this history has already entered a stage in which the arrival of the world near God, or the arrival in the world of God in his innermost reality, is already and irrevocably a fact. We might mention here that this was expressly asserted by the Second Vatican Council.

This meeting of God and world, which can no longer be nullified, is not only an event in the ultimate depths of created free subjects, it has also become manifest in collective history and, precisely in this way, has itself become irrevocable. This event of an historically borne, definitive unity of God (who freely communicates himself) and humanity (who freely accepts this communication) is called Jesus Christ, who died on the cross and rose from the dead. In Jesus Christ the dialogue between God and creature has reached an ultimate agreement that cannot be revoked. Because this Jesus is the unity between God's pledge and the acceptance of this pledge in faith, because Jesus always acts in an unbroken (by him) solidarity with individuals and with all humanity, this event of the indissoluble unity of God and world in Jesus is also a pledge of salvation for the whole of humanity.

In Jesus the irrevocable self-promise of God to the world, as the creative origin and ground of the cosmos and as its end that can really be reached in itself, has become a definitive event. It can no longer disappear from the world and its history. Thus in its eschatological irrevocability, it remains present in the indestructible community of those who believe: the Church. The Church is not just some kind of institution for the promotion of individual religiosity and virtuous living. She is first and last, in her faith, the sacramental presence of God's self-promise to the world, a promise that, from God's side, is forever victorious.

HOLY SCRIPTURE AS CONSTITUTIVE
OF THE PRIMITIVE COMMUNITY

Now we can finally arrive at an understanding of what we call Holy Scripture. This historical and irrevocable presence of the eschatological and irreversible salvific will of God has its origin in Jesus Christ and the primitive community around him. The historically continuing existence of this community of faith, as the presence of God's victorious salvation, is essentially related to the unique and unrepeatable event of the God-man and of the primitive community. Both of them remain forever the norm.

However, this does not mean that it was a particular religious phenomenon in the history of humanity, beside which other equally important phenomena and objectifications might exist. For Jesus and his original community are the event and the attestation of humanity's arrival near the infinite God, an arrival that is not merely a possibility but a reality. When we consider where humanity arrives, such an arrival has, of its very nature, no equivalent. And the historical attestation by Jesus Christ of this "having-arrived" has in fact, before him or next to him, no equivalent and it can have none after him, because beyond it nothing more can be said.

The primitive community given with Jesus, as the eschatological self-promise of God, must necessarily be constituted in the way in which such a community unavoidably had to have been constituted in its then cultural situation, and as it still has to be constituted, if it is to be the norm and the permanent standard for the faith community that continually renews itself generation after generation, as the sacramental salvific presence of God. This means concretely: One of the constitutive elements of this primitive community is a *book*. We say this without prejudging a further precision required by this statement, as will be shown later on.

In the cultural situation of humanity at that time, which had already reached the stage of writing and of putting together something like a book, a faith-community with a shared faith-consciousness is not conceivable except with the help of a book that has set down what is being believed and hoped. That book is a medium through which individuals communicate in their faith-consciousness, enabling them to constitute a unity. It is the medium of language and, at that time undoubtedly, also the medium of writing and of books. One of the constitutive factors of the primitive community of those who believe in Jesus is the book. This is true of this community in itself and of its function as norm for the future.

We must therefore consider this book as a constitutive element of the primitive community in its function of norm for all time to come. At the same time, this primitive community must be considered as the eschatological presence of God's promise of salvation irrevocably wrought by God's power. In this way, it seems to me that all that is being said about the Sacred Scripture of the Old and New Testaments — about God as the main author of Scripture, about inspiration, about Scripture as norm, about the inerrancy of Scripture — can be understood without recourse to the miraculous, which does not find credence today. It shows also how a reference to the sacred writings of other great cultural religions should not confuse Christians in their way of understanding the Holy Scriptures of Christianity.

HOLY SCRIPTURE — WORD OF GOD
AND WORD OF HUMAN BEINGS

The Second Vatican Council expressly emphasizes that the human authors of the Holy Scriptures truly composed these writings. They did not merely write what was dictated to them by God, who alone would be their "author." We may here ignore the question of whether a Catholic theology of Scripture after the Second Vatican Council is able to speak of verbal inspiration. God did not dictate the Scriptures in the usually understood sense of one person dictating to another. There was no need for God to feed statements into the consciousness of the writers through a miraculous intervention. If the human authors really wrote the Scriptures, God's authorship of Holy Scripture, which is a clear doctrine of our faith, must be understood in a way that does not imply that God composed them. Human beings composed the Scriptures. The fact that God is their author must mean something else.

We are entitled to say what follows: God, in his unchallenged and powerful grace, which does not cancel human freedom, causes the salvific event consisting of Christ and the primitive faith-community. God wills and guarantees that they will forever be the norm of faith. Now this primitive community cannot possibly exist nor be such a norm without the written objectification of its faith. If and insofar as this is true, it is also true that God is in a real way the author of Scripture, having already "inspired" it, and guarantees its "inerrancy" in the sense and with the limits that fit the proper task of Scripture. In other words: In the power of his grace God produces the primitive community. He produces it as a permanent norm for the future Church. He produces it as objectifying itself in special writings, which are the norm of the coming Church. In this way God produces these writings.

This leaves open all the possibilities of the individuality and freedom of the human composers in the primitive community as well as the fact that they were influenced by the situation in which they lived. These persons are the writers and their writings mirror their individuality. The writings originate through theological reflection on their experience of Jesus Christ, as the definitive and irrevocable self-promise of God in history. From the human point of view these writings often come into being fortuitously. They were not intentionally planned as a unity according to some basic system; they manifest a diversity of theological starting points, terminologies, and plausibilities. But even in their variety and differences they are valid witnesses to the faith of the primitive community. As such they were willed and brought forth by divine Providence, in God's perennial salvific grace, as the norm of faith for the coming Church throughout all generations.

Of course, besides the Scriptures transmitted to us, in the primitive community there were certainly other written objectifications of the faith of that community. Some of them would have been unfit to serve as normative objectifications of the faith of the primitive community, but others might have been accepted as such (for instance, the lost letters of Paul). The discernment made by the primitive community between written productions that would serve as norm and witness for later times and those that would not, in other words, the constitution and delimitation of the so-called canon of the Scriptures, must be attributed to the faith-instinct of the Church, as she moved from apostolic to post-apostolic times. We of later generations might notice that this discernment was very broadminded, and that as a result writings were admitted into the canon that we might not easily admit today. On the other hand, we might say that it was so strict that even today, despite their considerable differences in points of view and in Christian warmth and depth, all these writings constitute a genuine corpus of Scripture, serving as a lucid testimony of the Christian faith.

We must now say something about the Old Testament. Insofar as it was the Holy Scripture of Jesus, and as it belongs to the prehistory of Christianity and is acknowledged as such by the Christ-event, the Old Testament too belongs to the Holy Scriptures of Christianity. Christians discover it through Christ. Would we be able to discover it today as divinely produced Holy Scripture independently of Christ? Or would we, without Christ, consider it for our own existence and salvation only as a document of the history of religions, a document stemming from the Middle East, although a very important one, unsurpassed in ancient history? We will not try to answer this question.

The Old Testament is Holy Scripture for us, in the concrete situation of our faith and salvation, insofar as it was the Holy Scripture of Jesus, insofar as it "is about Christ." This does not deny the further religious significance of the Old Testament. It only emphasizes the fact that Christians arrive at it only through Jesus, that we must always read it with an eye on him who was crucified and rose from the dead. Although God's salvific will emerges and is already manifest in it, the Old Testament as such does not yet attest that this salvific will of God has come down to us, not as an ambivalent possibility of salvation, but as triumphant and irreversible. That is why it is rightly called the Old Testament.

Scripture is a human word, a human product, insofar as in it human beings bears witness that God is no longer the mysterious ground of a history that presses on into the unforeseeable future, but that God hastens to meet history as its absolute future and introduces it into his own infinity and luminous sovereignty. As human word, Scripture does not bear witness to what God, in his creative power, does here and there to finite reality. But Scripture is also God's word, and as God's word, it bears witness to God himself, as infinite gift to the world. Such an attestation is possible only if it is made by God himself, in a unique manner that goes beyond God's usual creative activity.

If Scripture did not, through God himself (through what we call the light of faith), bear witness to God, as a gift that victoriously makes its way, it would speak only of realities that are distinct from God, even if it spoke of them in their relation to God. In that case the content of its statements would not differ basically from content that, in principle, might also be reached by unaided human words. And then that essential difference from other human words, which Scripture itself attests, would no longer exist. Of course, this essential difference between Scripture as God's word and human words can ultimately be conceived and defended only if we grasp Scripture's essential relation to the cross and the resurrection of Jesus. For only in these eschatological salvific events is the triumph of God's self-promise to the world presented historically and therefore in words. The words of Scripture are, when we read them with faith, once more animated by this self-communication of God. Thus they are not only words about God (although authorized by God) and thus only human words. They are indeed words of God.

If Scripture is to be God's word reaching us and mediating God, it must, of course, also speak of humanity; it must also be human speech about humans. Thus human word about humanity has, in Scripture as elsewhere, diverse dimensions and degrees of binding force, in and with which human beings can speak about themselves and bear witness to themselves and their history. Thus much may be said in Scripture about humanity that may be important and, in some cases, remain forever valid for them. But all of this derives its ultimate binding power and importance from the fact that it happens in the context of the statement that God, in his infinity and absolute sovereignty, has not only offered himself to human beings, making possible their salvation, but also victoriously realizes this possibility. Every Christian anthropology that is intended to agree with Scripture should never forget this basic principle, and it should always remember that, because of human historicity, what it tells us about humanity does not always have the same degree of binding force.

HOLY SCRIPTURE AS A BOOK

Scripture as God's word, the Christian book of the Old and the New Testaments, was certainly, for all essentials, already present with and in the Church of apostolic times, that Church which is the lasting normative beginning of the eschatological stage of salvation history. But when we start speaking of the *book* of Holy Scripture, we should not overlook the fact that this book as a book has had a further history, in which its proper nature has been realized even more fully than before. Scripture is a message for all humanity and for each human person. This feature of Scripture is more radically realized, when it can immediately reach everybody everywhere. This has happened only since the time Scripture became a book that could be so easily reproduced that it could become everybody's book, that is, through the momentous breakthrough in our cultural history signified by the name Gutenberg.

Before the invention of printing Scripture existed, but not Scripture as *book* for *everyone.* That is Scripture's purpose, although, on the conscious level, the Catholic Church has clearly grasped this fact only through a long and laborious process, and said expressly, for the first time, in the Second Vatican Council that she wishes Scripture to be in everybody's hands. Formerly she treated Scripture almost like some secret writing that should be used only by experts in theology and in official preaching. It was only at the end of the fifteenth century that Scripture entered the stage of the full realization of its own nature. Every book, every library, every bookshop tells those for whom history derives its basic meaning from the fact that it is the salvation history of eternal life that the word of God, as incarnated in human words and hence in the written word, has reached the fullness of its nature.

Let us, at the end of these considerations, return once more to their start. The immense and breathtaking history of the cosmos derives its ultimate meaning from the fact that within this history there may emerge an immeasurable quantity of seemingly minute histories of spirit and freedom, in each of which the history of the cosmos comes to itself. And this history of spirit and freedom that occurs countless times as the coming-to-itself of the cosmos is at the same time the history of the self-communication of God as absolute future to this history of the freedom and the spirit of the cosmos.

The final outcome of this whole history of spirit and freedom, in which the cosmos comes to itself, and keeps striving for God, is called the everlasting kingdom of God. But in this history of the cosmos, of the spirit, and of freedom, the irrevocable victory of history is already attested and has already started. This beginning of the blessed fulfillment of the cosmos is called Jesus Christ, the one who passed through death to resurrection. The permanent presence of this victorious promise of God in Jesus Christ is called the Church of those who believe in Jesus, who love him and love God in him, and who, full of hope, die with him into the incomprehensibility of God.

Countless are the witnesses of this blessed fulfillment. In them the reality of what is attested is already present. Because of our bodily being God has provided an incarnational objectification of these witnesses. We call it Holy Scripture. It must, of course, be read with faith, else it would be only a human book that would perish in the fire of doomsday. Its word must ever and again be enacted in the sacramental word and in the word of preaching. However, because the history of humankind is not only human history but also the history of God (unconfused and undivided), there exist in it not only sculptures, buildings, poems, and books, in which human beings express their own nature in order to realize it, but also the man Jesus and his history, recorded in a book that must truly be called God's book, because in it God pledges himself to us as our eternal life.

LIST OF SOURCES

CONSCIENCE
Lecture delivered on 11 March 1983 in Vienna; published in
Orientierung 47 (1983) 246–50.

DIALOGUE AND TOLERANCE AS THE FOUNDATION
OF A HUMANE SOCIETY
Lecture delivered on 11 June 1983 in Pforzheim; published in
Stimmen der Zeit 201 (1983) 579–89.

UTOPIA AND REALITY:
THE SHAPE OF CHRISTIAN EXISTENCE
CAUGHT BETWEEN THE IDEAL AND THE REAL
Lecture delivered on 27 February 1983 in Bad Camberg; published
in *Geist und Leben* 56 (1983) 422–32, under the title "Christliche
Welt- und Lebensgestaltung zwischen Anspruch und Wirklichkeit."

THE THEOLOGICAL DIMENSION OF PEACE
Published in *Entschluss* 38 (3/1983) 11–13, under the title "Die
Offenheit auf Gott hin."

THE PROBLEM OF EUROPE'S FUTURE
Published in *Europa — Horizonte der Hoffnung*, edited by F. König
and K. Rahner (Graz, 1983), pp. 11–34

REALISTIC POSSIBILITY OF A UNIFICATION IN FAITH?
Lecture delivered on 20 January 1982 in Basel; published in *Das
Ringen um die Einheit der Christen: Zum Stand des evangelisch-
katholischen Dialogs*, edited by H. Fries (Dusseldorf, 1983),

225

pp. 176–92, under the title "Was kann realistischerweise Ziel der ökumenischen Bemühungen um die Einheit im Glauben sein?"; also in *Communicatio fidei: Festschrift für Eugen Biser*, edited by H. Bürkle and G. Becker (Regensburg, 1983), pp. 175–83; in part in *Evangelische Kommentare* 15 (1983) 480–84, under the title "Ökumenischer Realismus: Über das Ziel einer Einheit im Glauben."

CONCRETE OFFICIAL STEPS TOWARD UNIFICATION
Published in *Ökumene Möglichkeiten und Grenzen heute*, edited by K. Froehlich (Tubingen, 1982), pp. 80–85.

ECUMENICAL TOGETHERNESS TODAY
Published in *Quatember* 44 (1980) 3–12.

FORGOTTEN DOGMATIC INITIATIVES
OF THE SECOND VATICAN COUNCIL
Lecture delivered on 27 November 1982 in Freiburg; not previously published.

PERSPECTIVES FOR PASTORAL THEOLOGY
IN THE FUTURE
Published in *Diakonia* 12 (1981) 221–35.

THE FUTURE OF CHRISTIAN COMMUNITIES
Published in *Entschluss* 37 (12/1982), 11f., 16–20, under the title "Warum die Christen einer Minderheit bleiben."

RITES CONTROVERSY: NEW TASKS FOR THE CHURCH
Published in *Entschluss* 38 (7/8/1983) 28, 30f., under the title "Austausch statt Einbahn?"

THE RELATION BETWEEN THEOLOGY AND
POPULAR RELIGION
Published in *Volksreligion — Religion des Volkes*, edited by K. Rahner, C. Modehn, and M. Göpfert (Stuttgart, 1979), pp. 9–16, under the title "Einleitende Überlegungen zum Verhältnis von Theologie und Volksreligion."

SOUTH AMERICAN BASE COMMUNITIES
IN A EUROPEAN CHURCH
Published in *Entschluss* 36 (1/1981) 4–8.

CHRISTIAN PESSIMISM
Lecture delivered on 10 November 1983 in Frankfurt; previously unpublished.

WHAT THE CHURCH OFFICIALLY TEACHES AND
WHAT THE PEOPLE ACTUALLY BELIEVES
Published in *Theologie in Freiheit und Verantwortung*, edited by K. Rahner and H. Fries (Munich, 1981), pp. 15–29.

THEOLOGY AND THE ROMAN MAGISTERIUM
Published in *Stimmen der Zeit* 198 (1980) 363–75, under the title "Theologie und Lehramt."

THE PERENNIAL ACTUALITY OF THE PAPACY
Published in *Das Papsttum: Epochen und Gestalten*, edited by B. Moser (Munich, 1983), pp. 277–92, under the title "Paul VII. an Peppino — Ein Papstbrief aus dem 21. Jahrhundert."

UNDERSTANDING THE PRIESTLY OFFICE
Published in *Auf Wegen der Versöhnung: Beiträge zum ökumenischen Gespräch*, edited by P. Neuner and F. Wolfinger (Frankfurt, 1982), pp. 215–19, under the title "Kleine Randbemerkungen zur Frage des Amstverständnisses."

BOOK OF GOD — BOOK OF HUMAN BEINGS
Published in *Stimmen der Zeit* 202 (1984) 35–44, under the title "Die Heilige Schrift — Buch Gottes und Buch der Menschen."

INDEX